COFFIN SHIP

COFFIN SHIP

The Wreck
of the
Brig St. John

William Henry

MERCIER PRESS
IRISH PUBLISHER – IRISH STORY

MERCIER PRESS

Cork

www.mercierpress.ie

ISBN: 978 1 85635 631 2

10 9 8 7 6 5 4 3

A CIP record for this title is available from the British Library

Printed and bound in the EU.

In memory of
all who lost their lives at sea during
the Great Famine of 1845–1850

Their whitening bones in Atlantic deep
Have formed a living chain
Connecting their beloved land
With the land they sought in vain.

In God's house they dwell free from hunger
and destitution.

CONTENTS

ACKNOWLEDGEMENTS

This book would not have been possible without the persistence and research of John Bhaba Jaick Ó Congaola from Lettermullen, Connemara, who provided much of the research material so that the story of the brig *St. John* and the people who sailed on her will not be forgotten. One of the first people to highlight the plight of the *St. John* was the late Paddy Mulkerrin of Lettermullen, whose research is also included in this book. Sincere thanks also to Kathleen Berry for making me aware of this story. The poem 'To Their Memory' is from John Bhaba Jaick Ó Congaola's collection. Sincere thanks also to Noel McGuire, Gerry Joyce and St Anthony's and Claddagh Credit Union for their generous support.

Thanks also to the following: my wife Noreen, sons Patrick and David, and daughter Lisa, the National Library of Ireland, Dublin, the staff of the Clare County Library, Clare Local Studies Project, James Hardiman Library, NUIG, Galway County

Library, Island House, Michael Faherty, Marie Boran, Michael O'Connor, Geraldine Curtain, Anne Mitchell, Maureen Moran. To Patrick Henry, Friederike Angermeier, Colin Merrigan, John Costello, Brendan St John, Jack Meehan, John Sullivan, Johnny Bailey, Kieran Scanlon, P.J. Ui Fhlatarta, Pateen Mháirtin Ó Conghaile, Dermot Nestor, the St John family of Cohasset, the Comerford family of County Clare, the Ancient Order of Hibernians of America, the brig *St. John* committees of Lettermullen and Boston, and the Cohasset Maritime Museum for allowing John Bhaba Jaick Ó Congaola access to their files. To all in the media who gave excellent publicity to this project: Brendan Carroll, Dave Hickey, Stan Shields, Joe O'Shaughnessy, Margaret Blade, Ronnie O'Gorman, Dickie Byrne, Eamonn Howley, Tom Kenny, Keith Finnegan, Jimmy Norman, Tom Gilmore, Jim Carney, Mary Conroy, Peadar O'Dowd and Des Kelly. Special thanks to Peadar Ó Maoláin – Udarás na Gaeltachta, Cóiste an Bhrig Saint John – Leitir Mealláin, Cóiste an Bhrig Saint John – Boston, Ciarán Ó Scanláin, P.J. and Jacinta Ui Fhlatarta, Seán Folan, Máirtin Tom Sheáinin – Raídió na Gaeltachta, Macdara Ó Curraoin, Risteard Mac Aodha, Comhar Chuigéal, Mairéad Ní Chonghaile,

Tom Barrett, Conradh na Gaeilge – Gaillimh, Ann and Fachtna Mellotte.

Special thanks also to Kieran Hoare, James Casserly, Marita Silke, Tim Collins, Mark Kennedy, Liam Frehan, Mary Waller, Bill and Alice Scanlan, and Diarmuid Ó Cearbhaill for proofreading my work and making many valuable suggestions. Thanks to Bob Waller for his excellent work in reproducing photographs. Again I am deeply indebted to a very special friend, Jacqueline O'Brien, who has, as always, given so generously of her time both researching and proofreading, and for her expert advice, encouragement and support throughout this project.

The verse of the poem which appears on the dedication page is from a booklet entitled *Centenary Commemoration* (21-8-1949) which was published for the centenary of the disaster.

Note: Every effort has been made to acknowledge the sources of all the material used. Should a source not have been acknowledged, please contact Mercier Press and we will make the necessary corrections at the first opportunity.

PREFACE

Many books and stories have been written about the Great Famine, but few have illustrated the horrors as well as this, William Henry's latest book, *Coffin Ship: The Wreck of the Brig St. John.* In the lead-up to the central story of the tragic voyage, William Henry paints a picture of the conditions that prevailed in Ireland at the time, particularly at the emigrant port of Galway. He records the despair and desperation of the landless peasants, their often horrific journeys on foot to the famine ships and the callousness and dishonesty they suffered at the hands of the ship captains. He refers to the awful conditions which the emigrants endured in places such as Liverpool, where they were packed into small areas. William Henry does not write merely in general terms, but gives authenticity to the story by referring to individuals and their place of origin.

This excellent build-up gives way to the main story of one particular famine ship, the brig *St. John.* William Henry describes the characters of the captain and crew and outlines the difficulties of life on such a ship. He is at his best when outlining the mounting tension on board as desperate efforts are made to save the ship from the furious and unexpected storm.

In the aftermath of the tragedy, the William Henry maintains the reader's interest by relating the personal stories of both the passengers who survived the tragedy and those onshore who helped get them to safety. This is an outstandingly organised and unforgettable story.

James Casserly
President of the Old Galway Society, 2009

INTRODUCTION

The loss of the brig *St. John* off the coast of Massachusetts in October 1849 was one of the most tragic events to occur during the Great Famine of 1845–50. This book traces the last voyage of the brig *St. John*, and briefly recounts the story of some of those who sailed on her in an attempt to acquaint the reader with the human beings behind the statistics. It begins with a look at the background of the famine and includes eyewitness accounts from areas such as Skibbereen and Connemara. These accounts describe the horrific living conditions which left so many with little choice but to undertake the frightening and dangerous voyage overseas. It was the nightmarish and appalling conditions throughout the country that forced so many to take the path to a famine ship. The third chapter explores the conditions on board these coffin ships, focusing on several particularly shocking examples to highlight the sufferings of these people. The fourth chapter accompanies these people on their gruelling walk to the port, while the remaining chapters are devoted to the story of the *St. John*, its tragic end and aftermath. The book also includes a list of both the survivors and victims amongst the passengers and crew of the *St. John*.

The voyage to the New World was long and perilous. About one-fifth of those who sailed from Irish shores during the famine perished en route. Sources indicate that in 1847 alone, some 100,000 people set sail for British North America, with an estimated 20,000 of them either perishing aboard the 'coffin ships' or dying afterwards as a result of conditions on board. The remains of those who died from disease and hunger during the voyages were consigned to a sea grave. There was nothing to mark their final resting place.

The Irish peasants had worked long, hard hours in an exploitative landlord system. If they were unable to pay the extortionate rents demanded of them, they faced eviction. Bolstered by the police, the landlords' agents evicted many from their homes. The peasants' situation was exacerbated by a government that showed little interest in their plight. In the years before the famine the indifference and contempt of some members of the British government, expressed in their policies towards Ireland, had in a sense sealed the fate of the Irish people. Yet as famine ravaged the country, Ireland was being governed by the British Empire, a world superpower at the height of its glory.

However, not everyone turned a blind eye to the suffering of the Irish peasants. The Choctaw nation of North America, being no stranger to suffering and indifference itself, was moved to compassion by the plight of the Irish during the famine. In the winter of 1831, tens of thousands of Choctaws had been removed from their ancestral homelands in Mississippi and sent to a reservation in Oklahoma. The reason was that settlers and many other white Americans saw the Choctaw as standing in the way of progress and in their eagerness to secure land to raise cotton, they pressurised the federal government into forcibly acquiring the Choctaws' territory. During the forced march to the reservation, which became known as the 'Trail of Tears', almost half of the Choctaw people perished. The Choctaws raised $710 for the starving Irish, which would be equivalent to more than €100,000 in today's money.

Other groups also tried to help, among them the Society of Friends, or the Quakers as they are more commonly known. The Quakers donated consignments of flour, rice, biscuits and meal to the Irish people. Eventually soup kitchens replaced public works projects in Ireland and by 1847 this support was reaching some three million people on a daily basis.

Many older people still remember their parents being extremely conscientious regarding the wastage of food. I believe that this was a legacy from the famine passed down through successive generations. In a similar vein, for most Irish people it is an absolute priority that they have ownership of the house in which they live; it is embedded in the Irish mindset. This is another possible legacy from a period when evictions were the order of the day for those who could not afford to pay the rent.

I have been asked time and time again why I switched, midstream, from writing a series of children's books to writing about a tragedy such as the loss of the brig *St. John.* The original impetus for this book came from a dream. One night, while asleep in my bed, I found myself transported onto a nineteenth-century sailing ship. It was a beautiful sun-drenched day. I looked up at the sails as they fluttered gently in the warm breeze. I could feel the slow and gentle side-to-side motion of the ship as it floated on the waves. Moments later I became aware of movements ahead of me at the entrance to the hold of the ship. It was open and a sailor was slowly emerging from it, dragging a large object concealed by a white sheet along behind him. A second sailor stood to the rear of the first, and he was holding on to the other end of the sheet. The two sailors proceeded towards the gunwale of the ship where they emptied the contents of the sheet onto the deck.

I was shocked by what I saw – it was the lifeless, emaciated body of a man. It suddenly dawned on me that I was aboard a coffin ship. I had no idea how I had arrived there but for some reason I didn't question the strangeness of my surroundings. The sailors returned to the hold and repeated this same exercise several times over until a small heap of bodies lay on the deck. The sailors seemed oblivious to my presence as they lifted one of the bodies. One sailor grabbed the legs, while the other took the arms, and between them they raised the corpse onto the gunwale. They then dropped the body into the sea as though they were discarding nothing more than an old and worn pair of boots.

As they grabbed the next body, my emotions got the better of me and I shouted at them to have some respect, to say a prayer at least for these poor, wretched human beings. They didn't seem to hear me as they lifted a second body and consigned it to the sea. Advancing towards them I shouted, 'At least bless yourselves', but once again my cries fell on deaf ears. I looked down at one of the corpses still lying on the deck. Suddenly his head rolled around to face me. His eyes flew open and he looked directly at me in shock. I knew that he was aware of my presence. The sailors then grabbed him and threw his body over the side of the ship.

I ran and grabbed the gunwale and stared down at the sea. I was stunned. His body was floating about six inches below the surface of the water and his gaze was still fixed on me. It was then that I noticed he was not alone. As my eyes scanned the ocean I saw that there were literally thousands of other bodies floating alongside him. I was overcome by a mixture of sadness and fear. I heard him whisper the words 'Remember us, remember us', as he and all the other bodies slowly sank to the bottom of the ocean. On the second utterance of those haunting words I was sure I heard a chorus of other voices join in.

Suddenly I awoke and realised that it had all been a dream. I was drenched in sweat, but delighted to be safely back in my bed. My mind was a flurry of activity so, knowing there was little chance of returning to sleep, I began to process the dream. Such was the effect it had on me that the following morning I contacted a very gifted friend and spiritual Canadian woman called Naomi Jane Zettl to seek help in clarifying its meaning. Naomi is a woman of great wisdom and a short time later she informed me that one of the main messages of my dream was that something needed to be done to commemorate these people.

At the time I was not sure what to do but Naomi assured me that I would receive guidance and eventually her words made perfect sense. A few months later a woman, Kathleen Berry contacted me to write a book on the brig *St. John*, but at the time I was too busy. Later a man by the name of John Bhaba Jaick Ó Congaola, from Lettermullen, contacted me and also asked me to write a book on the brig *St. John*, as he believed I would be interested in the material. At the time I was still too busy to take on the project. Besides, I knew nothing about the *St. John*, let alone that it was a famine ship.

Over the following two years John Bhaba Jaick Ó

Congaola contacted me a number of times to write this book, but each time I declined. Then in July of 2008, being very persistent, he made a final attempt. He had other historical material that he believed would be of interest to me and he offered to give it to me along with the *St. John* material. Realising this book was not going to go away, I finally agreed to examine the material. I was taken aback by the content: one document stated that if a timber headstone had been placed on the ocean for every man, woman and child consigned to a watery grave during the famine, the tombstones would have extended from Cobh in Cork to Boston Harbour. I was stunned; a shiver ran up along my spine and the hair stood up on the back of my neck. The dream from two years earlier came hurtling back to me.

Some might say that my dream and this material being delivered to me are nothing more than co-incidence, and who could blame them. But all I can say is that you would have to have been there and felt what I felt and saw what I saw to realise that this was more than just a coincidence. I can honestly say that I did not intentionally set out to write this book. It sought me out on five occasions, and thank God that this book, in a sense, chose me.

I

THE GREAT FAMINE

It may prove difficult for those who have not studied nineteenth-century Irish history to understand why so many thousands of people, in fleeing their country, risked dying from starvation or disease on board a coffin ship. This hazardous journey across the Atlantic Ocean was often undertaken on overcrowded and unsafe ships. The Great Famine, which devastated Ireland between the years 1845 and 1850, was one of the most tragic events in Irish history. It left an estimated one million people dead, although the true figure will never be known. At least another one million people fled to other countries in the hope of a better life.

A potato riot in Galway in 1842.
(The Illustrated London News)

Outbreaks of famine were not uncommon in Ireland at the time. During the previous century, potato crops had failed on a number of occasions. On the last day of the year 1739, Ireland awoke to find itself in the grip of what could be termed a mini Ice Age. This severe winter was followed by a summer of famine and disease during which a large number of peasants perished. Many parts

Boy and girl foraging for potatoes on the road to Cahera, County Cork.
(The Illustrated London News, 20-2-1847)

Miss Kennedy distributing clothing in Kilrush, County Clare.
(The Illustrated London News, 22-12-1849)

of Ireland suffered. One report stated that 'the dead have been eaten in the fields by dogs for want of people to bury them'. Food shortages were reported again in 1816 and 1817. In 1822 Galway was already suffering from the effects of poverty and high unemployment, and the failure of the potato crop that year caused a minor famine. Hordes of people flocked to the city in search of food, but the town was already struggling to feed its own population. During the summer, fever was widespread, and grants were made available by the local authorities to combat the epidemic. By November, the scourge seems to have passed. Other food shortages occurred in 1831 and 1842; the latter resulting in food riots in Galway city where potato stores were attacked. However, the catastrophe of the Great Famine that swept across Ireland in 1845 was incomparable to anything the country had ever witnessed before.[1]

The devastation of the famine has its origins in the introduction of the Penal Laws of 1695. These unjust laws deprived the Catholic majority of many civil rights in areas such as education, religious freedom and ownership of land, and paved the way for the rise of the Protestant ascendancy class. These landed gentry families exerted an almost limitless power over their tenants. Many were absentee landlords living in England who had little interest in their property except to make as much profit from their tenants as possible. Rents were high and if the tenants could not raise the necessary finance, they faced eviction. The saving grace for the Irish peasant was the potato, as it was cheap to produce, easy to cultivate and yielded large crops. The potato was also a good source of vitamins.

At the time the population of Ireland was about eight million. Tenant housing consisted mainly of small thatched buildings or small one-roomed huts constructed of stone or sometimes turf. While both buildings were very basic, the huts were dreadful places to live. They had no windows or chimney, just a hole in the roof to allow the smoke from the fire to escape. Infant mortality was high because of such impoverished living conditions. Given the rigid land division and landlord policies, the vast majority of the Catholic population were forced to live on the brink of starvation and destitution on an ongoing basis.

Once the potato crop was planted, the tenants were then free to 'work off' their rent on the landlord's estate. The situation was such that in 1843 the Devon Commission, having examined the Irish economic system, reported that the landlords and their policies were the main cause of the widespread poverty amongst the people. One member stated that the Irish people were the 'worst fed, worst clothed, but were the most patient people in Europe'.[2]

In June 1845, frightening reports began arriving from Europe that a new blight called *Phytophthora infestans* had been detected in Belgium. It was not

The Macedonian sails into Cork with provisions for Ireland.
(The Illustrated London News, 7-8-1847)

known where the blight had originated but it was
suspected to have come from South America two years
earlier, perhaps carried to Europe in fertiliser. On 9
September 1845, the *Dublin Evening Post* reported
that the curator of the Botanic Gardens in Glasnevin,
David Moore, had stated that specimens of potatoes
sent to him from Wexford and Waterford showed

Searching for potatoes in a stubble field in County Clare.
(The Illustrated London News, 22-12-1849)

'convincing proofs of the rapid progress this alarming disease is making. Some of the stems looked fertile, but when dug up the roots were rotten.'

Reports from Mayo said that an 'intolerable stench' filled the air during the digging of potato crops. That same year, thousands of people died from starvation in France, the Netherlands, Germany and Switzerland because of huge crop failures. However, people living in these areas were not as dependent on the potato as the Irish and so the stage was set for disaster.

The rest of Europe was spared further fatalities when a year later a severe drought helped kill off the blight, thus avoiding the catastrophe that befell Ireland. The following statistics indicate the extent of the Irish famine: the blight destroyed one-third of the potato crop in 1845, three-quarters in the years 1846 and 1847, and one-third in 1849.[3]

Charles Edward Trevelyan, who was the permanent secretary of the British Treasury during the famine, worked hard on introducing relief schemes that generated employment in the area of road construction and repair. However, Trevelyan was against the idea of dispensing free aid and his attitude to the Irish was appalling. He believed that the famine was God's way of punishing an idle, ungrateful and rebellious nation.

By November 1846, with food prices on the increase, a labourer had to earn twenty-one shillings a week to sustain an average-sized family. Even if one was fortunate enough to secure work on a relief scheme, wages were still only between six and eight shillings a week. Families hadn't enough money to feed themselves and they were becoming increasingly malnourished all the time; this was a recipe for disaster. It was not as though the authorities were not informed of the imminent dangers. In a letter to Trevelyan dated August 1846, Fr Theobald Mathew wrote:

A blast has passed over the land, and the food of a whole nation has perished. On the 27th of last month I passed from Cork to Dublin, and this doomed plant bloomed in all luxuriance of an abundant harvest. Returning on the third instant, I beheld, with sorrow, one wide waste of putrefying vegetation. In many places the wretched people were seated on the fences of their decaying gardens, wringing their hands and wailing bitterly the destruction that had left them foodless.[4]

Bridget O'Donnell and her two children, County Clare.
(The Illustrated London News, 22-12-1849)

When one considers the ongoing exportation of food, the tenant evictions and the poor travelling conditions on offer to those fleeing the country, it is reasonable to say that a serious lack of concern for the Irish people existed. While the government received ample warning of the seriousness of the situation in Ireland, they simply failed to take adequate action. In fact, even as the disaster was unfolding the British Prime Minister, Sir Robert Peel, stated, 'there is such a tendency to exaggeration and inaccuracy in Irish reports that delay in acting upon them is always desirable'.

The following letter, published in the *Galway Mercury* in July 1847, challenged the 'absolute rubbish' being 'peddled' by politicians in relation to the hidden treasures of the Irish peasantry:

> *Of all the wonderful discoveries in this age of invention there cannot be found one so remarkable as that lately set before the public, by the Prime Minister of England, in relation to this unfortunate country. Two or three years ago Lord Stanley astonished the world by announcing, what he declared to be a well-ascertained fact, that the Irish peasantry were possessed of heaps of hidden treasure – that they had*

hoarded up wealth, and that money, in all shapes, could be found in their coffers. But what was this to the assertion of the noble member for London, lately made in the high court of parliament, namely, THAT THERE WERE VERY FEW DEATHS FROM STARVATION IN IRELAND?

No doubt, in the estimation of the very great, though withal very insignificant Statesman, the deaths have been by no means on as extensive a scale as he could wish – no doubt his policy was intended to produce a far more wide-spread mortality. It is not his fault if no more than two millions of human beings shall not in the course of a single year, be sacrificed in Ireland, to the doctrines of political economy – but why mock our sufferings? – why torture us still further by the cruel assertion which he has just sent forth, as if to prevent the flow of public sympathy towards alleviating the miseries of our wretched people. When men read these things abroad – when Europeans and Americans shall peruse the proceedings in Parliament, they will naturally say to themselves that matters are not so bad in Ireland as was represented, that plenty is flowing in, and disease going forth from the land.

> *Well, truly, we are a misgoverned race, when a person entrusted with the conduct of public affairs could dare to make such an assertion. How forcibly does this prove to us the folly of submitting any longer to be ruled by men so utterly ignorant, or wilfully blind to the interests of this portion of the Empire?*[5]

Were these sentiments intended to ease the conscience of a government refusing to face up to its responsibilities? Some would say that more sinister motives were at play; that a natural disaster was allowed to develop, through starvation, destitution, disease, fever and mass emigration.

II

A SHOCKING ACCOUNT

The scepticism on the part of some politicians about the extent of the problem in Ireland proved extremely costly for the country, and the high price paid by the unfortunate people can neither be ignored nor forgotten.

In 1847, the *Illustrated London News* reported that accounts from the Irish provincial papers continued to detail the terrible sufferings of the starving peasantry in Ireland. The artist James Mahoney from Cork, who was working for the *Illustrated London News* at the time, recounted his experiences in the newspaper. His journey began in Cork city; his destination was Skibbereen. One of the worst hit areas in Ireland

Old Chapel Lane, Skibbereen, County Cork.
(The Illustrated London News, 13-2-1847)

during the famine was Skibbereen in County Cork. 'Remember Skibbereen' became a byword for rebels in the years following the famine; in fact it is occasionally still uttered today. He encountered few problems during the journey until he reached Clonakilty, where he stopped for breakfast. It was here that the horrors of poverty first became visible to him. Vast numbers of 'famished poor' flocked around the coach and began begging. Among them was a woman carrying the corpse of a small child in her arms. She was making the most distressing appeal to the passengers for aid to 'enable her to purchase a coffin and bury her dear little baby'. Upon enquiring at the hotel, Mahoney was informed that each new day brought 'dozens' more destitute and starving people to the town.[1]

Upon leaving Clonakilty, Mahoney encountered yet more evidence of misery. He recorded meeting a funeral party almost every hundred yards. This continued until he reached an area close to the Shepperton Lakes. Here, the distress became even more striking. When he reached Skibbereen, he stayed at the residence of Mr J. McCarthy-Dowling. It was while at this location that he met with Dr D. Donovan and his assistant, Mr Crowley. Dr Donovan had been recording the devastation caused by the famine in his diary. He was also publishing extracts from the diary in the *Cork Southern Reporter*, yet people remained doubtful that such devastation in the countryside could be true. Accompanied by these two men, Mahoney visited areas around Skibbereen. He recorded that 'neither pen nor pencil could ever portray the misery and horror, at this moment, to be witnessed in Skibbereen'. Dr Donovan then accompanied Mahoney to Bridgetown where, upon arrival, they witnessed even worse sights. On visiting one particular house Mahoney noted that the dying, the living and the dead were indiscriminately lying close to each other with nothing to protect themselves, save a few miserable rags that served as clothing. Some of the dead remained scattered amongst the living for up to six days at a time; such was the level of weakness and fear of disease that family members delayed so long in burying their loved ones. These scenes were commonplace; all the houses contained similar horrors. No family was spared. Of some five hundred houses, not one was free from death or fever.

Mahoney and Dr Donovan proceeded to High Street or Old Chapel Lane where they came upon a house with neither doors nor windows. It was filled with destitute people lying on the bare floor. Amongst them was the body of a 'fine, tall, stout country lad', who had sought shelter from the piercing cold. The witnesses felt sure that the other occupants of the house would soon join him in death. It was a heart-rending sight and Mahoney and the other members of their group instinctively wanted to help alleviate the dreadful situation. But Dr Donovan became alarmed

Tim Harrington's hut, County Cork.
(The Illustrated London News, 13-2-1847)

that they would put themselves at risk of infection and
he pleaded with them not to enter the house and to
avoid physical contact with the people gathered in the
doorway.[2] Their next stop was at the Chapel yard. The

Funeral at Skibbereen, County Cork.
(The Illustrated London News, 13-2-1847)

following extract, taken from the diary of Dr Donovan, describes what they encountered:

> *On my return home, I remembered that I had yet a visit to pay; having in the morning received a ticket to see six members of one family, named Barrett, who had been turned out of the cabin in which they lodged, in the neighbourhood of Old Chapel yard; and who had struggled to this burying-ground, and literally entombed themselves in a small watch-house that was built for the shelter of those who*

were engaged in guarding against exhumation by
the doctors, when more respect was paid to the dead
than is at present the case. This shed is exactly seven
feet long, by about six in breadth. By the side of the
western wall is a long, newly made grave; by either
gable are two of shorter dimensions, which have
been recently tenanted; and near the hole that serves
as a doorway is the last resting-place of two or three
children; in fact, this hut is surrounded by a rampart
of human bones, which have accumulated to such a
height that the threshold, which was originally on
a level with the ground, is now two feet beneath
it. In this horrible den, in the midst of a mass of
human putrefaction, six individuals, males and
females, labouring under most malignant fever,
were huddled together, as closely as were the dead in
the graves around.

At the time (eleven o'clock at night) that I went
to visit these poor sufferers, it was blowing a perfect
hurricane, and such groans of roaring wind and rain
I never remember to have heard. I was accompanied
by my assistant, Crowley, and we took with us
some bread, tea and sugar; on reaching this vault, I
thrust my head through the hole of [the] entrance,

and had immediately to draw back, so intolerable
was the effluvium; and, though rendered callous by
a companionship for many years with disease and
death, yet I was completely unnerved at the humble
scene of suffering and misery that was presented to
my view; six fellow creatures were almost buried
alive in this filthy sepulchre. When they heard my
voice, one called out, 'Is that the Priest?' another, 'Is
that the Doctor?' The mother of the family begged in
the most earnest manner that I would have them
removed, or else that they would rot together; and
they all implored that we would give them drink.
Mr Crowley produced the tea and sugar, but they
said it was of no use to them, as they had no fire or
place to light it in, and that what they wanted was
water; that they had put a jug under the droppings
from the roof, but would not have drink enough for
the night. The next day I got the consent of the Poor
Law Guardians to have my patients removed from
this abode of the dead to the fever hospital, and they
are since improving.[3]

James Mahoney proceeded to enlist the help of a Mr
Everett, who had a great knowledge of the countryside.

Woman begging at Clonakilty, County Cork.
(The Illustrated London News, 13-2-1847)

During their journey they visited a hut where four people had lain dead for six days; it was the abode of a Tim Harrington. On hearing their voices, Mr Harrington made an effort to reach the door, and he asked for a drink of water and a fire to keep him warm. He collapsed in the doorway and in all probability died

Funeral at Shepperton Lakes, County Cork.
(The Illustrated London News, 13-2-1847)

as they were unable to give him aid through fear of contracting disease. Mahoney and Everett continued on to Schull where they encountered a group of over three hundred women looking to purchase food. Some had queued from daybreak to buy Indian meal from government-appointed officers. The officers appeared to be issuing 'miserable quantities' at high 'famine prices'. Mahoney's harrowing reports were published in their entirety in the Irish newspapers as well as the *Illustrated London News*, and should rightly have inspired an urgent response from the government.[4]

Another two men to publish reports on the devastating effects of the famine were Mr Forster and his son from Leeds. They visited Connacht in January 1847 on behalf of their community, to view 'first-hand' the devastation caused by the famine. The following is an extract taken from their report on the village of Bunderagh in Connemara:

> *One poor woman, whose cabin I had visited, said, 'There will be nothing for us but to lie down and die.' I tried to give her hope of English aid, but, alas, her prophecy has been too true. Out of a population of 240, I found 13 already dead from want. The survivors were like walking skeletons – the men gaunt and haggard, stamped with the livid mark of hunger – the children crying with pain – the women in some of the cabins too weak to stand.*

On the way to Clifden, Foster and his son came across around one hundred men engaged in famine-relief road works near Kylemore. Many of them had to walk between five and seven miles every day and earned a mere four shillings and sixpence per week. They had only one meagre meal a day to sustain them during this 'back-breaking' stonework. A policeman who was standing close by told the visitors that some of the men work 'till they fall over their tools' such was their weakened state.

Upon arriving in Clifden they were confronted with further harrowing sights close to where they were staying. A woman who had crawled into an outhouse on the previous night had died. By the time her body was found, part of her remains had been devoured by dogs. That same evening they observed another corpse being pushed through the streets in a wheelbarrow by a man desperately seeking assistance in burying the body. The following morning Foster and his son left for Galway. Along the way they encountered emaciated women and children, who were almost naked despite the brutal winter conditions.

As they journeyed throughout Connemara, the question on their minds was not how these people died but rather how they lived. They had anticipated that the situation in Connacht would be bad but nothing could have prepared them for the absolute desolation that greeted them, a desolation that 'defied all exaggeration'.[5]

One can see from these reports why the coffin ships might have seemed an attractive option, even a salvation, despite the terrible stories that surrounded the voyages. There had been emigration before the famine, but not on the scale witnessed during the famine years and the decades that followed. In contrast to previous emigration, when it was largely young men and women who left the country, children and elderly people constituted a large percentage of those who fled during the famine. Many of them had been weakened by fever and starvation long before the voyage.

Passenger companies took advantage of the desperate situation. They encouraged mass emigration through newspaper advertisements that promised an escape from the horrors sweeping across the land. Many emigrants were packed into the lower decks like 'slaves in a slave ship' and confined without light or fresh air during bad weather, making these ships fertile ground for the spread of disease. In the initial stages of the famine, America responded well with aid, but the sudden influx of starving and impoverished emigrants, many of whom were too weak to work, appalled the American authorities. They enforced Passenger Acts which resulted in some ships being turned away from American ports; for these people all hope was lost.[6]

The following poem appeared in the *Illustrated London News* on 13 February 1847:

Uncoffin'd, unshrouded, his bleak corpse they bore,
From the spot where he died on the Cabin's wet
    floor,
To a hole which they dug in the garden close by;
Thus a brother hath died – thus a Christian must
    lie!

'Twas a horrible end to a harrowing tale,
To chill the strong heart – to strike revelry pale.
No disease o'er this Victim could mastery claim,
'Twas Famine alone marked his skeleton frame!

The bones of his Grandsire and Father too, rest
In the old Abbey-yard, by the holy rites blest;
Their last hours were sooth'd by affections' fond
    cares,
Their last sighs were breath'd midst their Friends'
    tearful prayers!

Unshriven, untended, this man pass'd away,
Ere Time streak'd one hair of his dark locks with
    gray,
His requiem the wild wind, and Ilen's hoarse roar,
As its swollen waves dash on the rock-girded shore.

III

COFFIN SHIPS

The term 'coffin ship' is mainly given to vessels that carried Irish emigrants overseas during the famine of 1845-1850. Many of these ships were freight vessels that had been converted for carrying passengers. In some cases the ships were old sailing vessels which merchants no longer trusted with valuable cargos. Every inch of space was utilised to accommodate hastily built improvised bunks. This meant that in many cases the ships were overloaded beyond the limits of safety. The conditions in the lower compartments were exceptionally terrible.

Those who could not afford the ship fare would gather at the ports and offer what meagre savings

The emigrant ship, Artemisia.
(The Illustrated London News, 12-8-1848)

they had to sailors in order to gain access to the ships. Others, particularly young people, would sometimes stowaway on departing ships.

Many passengers were already weakened by hunger and were suffering from malnutrition and other famine-related illnesses. Yet some shipowners provided as little food and water as possible; working just inside the legal requirements, if indeed they obeyed the law at all. These ships were often overcrowded and disease-ridden and people endured terrible hardship on the long sea voyages. However, they were the cheapest way of crossing the Atlantic and the only way of escaping the horrors of the famine. Many ships were often short of manpower and during storms weak and hungry male passengers would be forced to lend a hand and do the work of a sailor.[1]

Food was scarce and at times emigrants had to supply their own rations. The situation for some emigrants was deplorable; having paid the fare, which cost either £3 or £3-10s, they were left with little or no money to purchase food. They then had to rely on the charity of fellow passengers, those better off than themselves. In some cases passengers were thought of as little more than ballast for the ships, and sadly, the remains of those who died during the voyage were consigned to the bottom of the sea. There are horror stories of sharks following ships because of the plentiful supply of bodies they were guaranteed.

Ship operators frequently smuggled additional passengers on board and as these people were not listed in the ship's manifest, it is impossible to determine exactly how many lives were lost to the sea. Emigrants did the cooking themselves and this was an ordeal in

Departure of an emigrant ship.
(The Illustrated London News, 6-7-1850)

itself, with passengers forced to queue for hours to use the small stoves available on the open deck. Those who had fallen ill depended on others to procure their meagre rations. Drinking water was usually in short supply, adding to the suffering.

In favourable conditions the voyage to America would take about six to eight weeks, but during bad weather, such as storms and gales, the journey could take as long as twelve weeks.[2]

Some landlords used the famine as an opportunity to clear their land of tenants who could no longer work and were becoming a burden, by paying for their passage to Canada and the United States. The following is just a sample of the loss of life during the Atlantic journeys. In July 1846, the *Elizabeth and Sarah* sailed from County Mayo, bound for Canada. There were 276 passengers on board, but only 212 were listed in the ship's manifest. To sustain these people with fresh water for the duration of the journey there should have been 12,532 gallons in storage, however, the ship carried only 8,700 gallons. Each passenger was entitled to 7 lbs of provisions per week, but in this case none were issued. The unfortunate people had to depend on the meagre rations they had managed to acquire before leaving Ireland. The journey took eight weeks, during which forty-two people died.

In 1847, the *Lord Ashburton* was inspected at Grosse Île, Canada, and was labelled a 'disgrace to the home authorities'. It seems that 107 passengers had died during the journey from Ireland.

In August of 1847, the *Virginius* sailed with 476 passengers. Conditions were so appalling on board that 158 of them died during the voyage. The filth and dirt

Between the decks of an emigrant ship.
(The Illustrated London News, 17-8-1850)

on board some of these vessels created such an 'effluvium as to make it hard to breathe'. Corpses were sometimes dragged up on deck using boat hooks as even relatives of the dead were fearful of being contaminated by disease. Sometimes sheets were used to remove the dead and convey them to their last resting place, the sea. Having reached their destination, people continued to die in their droves. The *Agnes* arrived in Canada with 427 passengers. After being held in quarantine for fifteen days, only 150 people were still alive.[3]

There was also the danger that a ship might sink en route and lose its entire complement of passengers and crew. Between 1847 and 1853, some fifty-nine emigrant ships sank while making the journey to America. Among them was the *Exmouth Castle*, which resulted in even more deaths than the loss of the *St. John*. The ship departed from the port of Derry on 25 April 1847 and was bound for Quebec, Canada. The vessel was registered to carry 165 passengers; but with two children being counted as one adult, there may have been as many as 240 on board. As the ship lost sight of land a light breeze began to blow, and by midnight it had turned into a storm. The storm increased in violence and lasted for several days. The brig fought for survival until eventually, on 28 April, having been driven back by the sheer force of the storm, it struck rocks off the coast of Scotland and sank. Only three sailors survived. In June 1848, the *Commerce* went down with sixty-eight passengers off Port Manton Island, Nova Scotia. On 24 August 1848, the *Ocean Monarch* sank off Liverpool resulting in 178 of its 306 emigrants being lost. The paddle steamer,

The wreck of the Mary Elizabeth.
(The Illustrated London News, 22-9-1849)

Londonderry, ran into trouble while ferrying people from Derry to Liverpool in 1848. It was the first leg of their journey to America. A sudden storm battered the steamer and the captain gave orders that all passengers were to be locked into a cabin below deck for the duration of the storm. The compartment was much too small to accommodate the 174 passengers and they struggled for air throughout the night. While some were crushed, others suffocated. By the time the

The wreck of the Floridion.
(The Illustrated London News, 10-3-1849)

doors were opened the following morning 31 women, 23 men and 18 children had lost their lives. On 2 January 1849, the *Cushlamachree* sailed out of Galway, bound for New York. The ship was owned by Patrick Lynch of Galway and was carrying 119 passengers. The *Cushlamachree* met with terrible weather conditions from the very beginning and the passengers had to endure a the majority of the brutal eight-week voyage

For the Flourishing City of NEW-YORK.

THE SPLENDID NEW BARQUE
HELENA,
F.I.,
Copper-fastened, 800 Tons Burthen,
JOHN H. BERRELL,
Commander,

Will Sail for the above City (weather permitting) on the 25th day of APRIL instant.

This fine Vessel made her passage to North America last season in the unprecedented time of fourteen days, one of the quickest passages known to be made across the Atlantic by a sailing vessel. The accommodation for Cabin and Steerage Passengers will be commodious and comfortable. She will be amply provided with Provisions, Fuel, and Water. Every possible attention will be paid to the comfort of the passengers during the voyage by the Captain and Crew.

For Freight or Passage apply to James Fitzgerald, Back-street; Edward Duffy, Back-street, Galway, or to the Captain on board.   Galway, 1st April, 1848.

For the Flourishing City of BALTIMORE.

THE SPLENDID NEW BARQUE
ALBION,
800 Tons Burthen,
JOHN TURNER, Commander,

Will Sail for the above City (weather permitting) on the 15th APRIL inst.

This fine Vessel made her passage to New York last season in twenty days. Her accommodations for Cabin and Steerage Passengers will be commodious and comfortable. She will be amply provided with Provisions, Fuel, and Water. Every possible attention will be paid to the comfort of the Passengers during the voyage by the Captain and Crew.

The Passengers going out by this Ship will be given a Certificate by the United States' Consul here, Mr. THOMAS PERSSE, which will provide them with immediate employment on their arrival in America.

Any person whose passage has been paid by their friends in America are requested to apply early for their berths.

For Freight or Passage apply to Robert D. Persse, Dominick-street, Edmond Duffy, Back-street, Galway, or the Captain on board, at the New Dock,

Galway, 8th April, 1848

Advertisements for emigrant ships Helena *and* Albion *out of Galway in 1848.*
(The Galway Mercury, 8-4-1848)

in the overcrowded hold, arriving in New York on 1 March 1849. While no passengers were lost, they never forgot the hardship and frightening experience of this crossing.[4]

While the above stories are horrific, they fall short of relating the day-to-day hardships endured by individuals, which were shocking beyond words. Mothers watched their children die, almost too scared to hold them lest they contract disease. They later watched as their pitiful emaciated remains were dropped into the sea. Such scenes had become commonplace.

While summer sailings presented their own set of sufferings, winter sailings were horrendous, with icy cold winds compounding the misery of the passengers. Some years after the famine, Dr Curtis, from Dublin, who was a former ship's surgeon, wrote, 'The torments of hell, might, in some degree, resemble the sufferings of the emigrants on these ships.'

Those who survived the coffin ship voyages carried terrifying stories of the journey ashore upon arriving at their destination. The high mortality rate among passengers was evident and the survivors' stories shocked and frightened many people. To counteract

Indian Corn, Meal, Biscuit, &c., &c.

R. D. PERSSE

Has this day arrived to him, per "The Cushlamachree," Thomas, Master, from New York, 400 Tons Yellow Indian Corn, 50 Boxes Soda Biscuit, 50 Barrels Navy do., and 10 Barrels Beans and Peas, Which, with 1200 Barrels Best American Flour, will be sold on the most moderate terms.

Merchants-road, Galway, June 15, 1847.

For the Flourishing City of ST. JOHN'S, N.B

The Splendid New Copper Fastened Ship,

CUSHLAMACHREE,

OF GALWAY,

Captain, JOHN THOMAS, 500 Tons Burden, will Sail for the above Port on the 29th inst. (wind and weather permitting). This Ship has just arrived from New York in the short space of Twenty Days; she will sail on the day appointed, and will be fitted up in a superior manner for the accommodation of Cabin and Steerage Passengers. A great many passengers are already engaged for this favourite Ship, so that early application will be necessary to the Captain on Board, at the New Dock, or to

EVANS & SONS, Ship Brokers, Galway.

Galway June 16th, 1847.

For ST. JOHN'S, N.B.

The Fast Sailing Copper Fastened Brig, "ALICE," OF GALWAY,

500 Tons Burden.

Captain GEORGE M'KAY,

Will Sail for the above Port on the 3d JULY next (wind and weather permitting).

THIS splendid New Ship belongs to Galway, and will be fitted up with every requisite to ensure the comfort of Passengers, and will be provided with Fuel and Water, and One Pound of Meal or Bread per day will be allowed to each Passenger, according to Act of Parliament.

The Captain, being long acquainted with the Passenger Trade, will afford Emigrants all necessary information on their arrival.

As several have already secured berths, early application is necessary to Messrs. Rush & Palmer, Dominick-street; Mr. R. N. Somerville, Eyre-square; Malachy Mannion, Bohermore; or John Lydon, Upper Dominick-street.

Galway, June 16th, 1847.

Advertisements for emigrant ship, Cushlamacree.
(The Galway Mercury, 18-6-1847)

The deck of the Artemisia.
(The Illustrated London News, 12-8-1848)

such stories, shipowners published accounts of successful voyages in newspapers. Henry Comerford, co-owner of the brig *St. John,* placed the following notice in the *Galway Mercury* in January 1847:

> ... *the failure of the potato crop in Ireland will considerably increase the demand for labour in America, upon which poor Ireland has principally to rely for receiving a supply of food ... There can*

be no doubt, whatever, of obtaining immediate employment and high wages.[5]

Most people did not trust these reports; however, true or untrue, the coffin ships were the only way of escaping the famine. Obviously some ships were better than others; this could also be said of the captains and their crews. The more superior ships had more than one emigrant deck and would have been considerably healthier. The following letter of acknowledgement was written in 1847 by Michael Burke and John Geoghegan, and sent to Captain Stitt of the *Midas*:

At the request of our fellow passengers, in all 190 souls, we beg to return you our sincere and heart-felt thanks for your kind and fatherly attention to all our wants and comforts during the voyage, in giving us all full share of provisions and plenty of water, and medicine late and early when required, and your constant attention on all occasions for which we shall be ever grateful and an account of which we have written to our friends in poor old Ireland.[6]

Humane Society Medal awarded after the sinking of the
Ocean Monarch *off Liverpool.*
(The Illustrated London News, 28-10-1848)

IV

A GRUELLING WALK

Most of the people intending to sail away from
Galway on the brig *St. John* in 1849 would have had
to walk to the port. The majority of them would have
had no previous experience of a sea voyage, but the
St. John was now their only hope of salvation. During
the journey from County Clare and Connemara, these
people experienced the full devastation of famine and
disease. Epidemics of typhus and relapsing fever raged
and were carried along by those fleeing stricken areas.
Many deaths were caused by outbreaks of dysentery,
diarrhoea, measles and tuberculosis, as malnutrition
had weakened the immune systems of the starving.
The stench of blight and death clung to the clothes

Spailpín of Tim Downs at Dunmore in County Clare.
(The Illustrated London News, 22-12-1849)

of these wretched people. The land of their birth, and that of their forefathers, had now forsaken them, allowing death to reap a rich harvest of corpses across the country. There was no age limit; young and old perished together. Their back-breaking toil had been in vain, their only hope of salvation was relief work, the workhouse or the coffin ships. Whole families –

grandparents, fathers, mothers and children – trudged along the old dirt roads towards the harbour towns. Scourged by hunger, bare-footed and dressed in rags, they wondered why this dreaded curse had been inflicted upon them, many tilting their heads towards the sky and calling out to heaven for answers.[1]

The scale of exodus was enormous, with thousands making this same journey throughout Ireland. Hundreds died along the way, and were left lying in ditches along the side of the road, their grass-stained mouths bearing testament to their desperation. One particular case was that of Pat and Bridget Duffy, a brother and sister who lived near Spiddal in County Galway. The only food they could find during the days leading up to their deaths, if one could call it food, was 'sea grass and sea weed'.

There was little hope of finding sustenance during the exhausting walk to the ports, so those fleeing carried their own meagre supplies with them. Any possessions of value had already been exchanged for food, or sold off for the price of a ticket to America or Canada. Some portable possessions were taken and used to barter along the way. In towns and villages the inhabitants shunned them out of fear of disease,

Village on Movren, County Clare.
(The Illustrated London News, 22-12-1849)

so terrified were they by horrific sights they had witnessed. Compassion for the poor and destitute was tenuous; people were so terrified of contracting disease that, having refused a beggar assistance, they would label them false and better off than they claimed just to assuage their own consciences.

While Galway was by no means the worst hit area during the famine, it did suffer its share of disease, starvation and death. It was once said of Rahoon that no language could express the ghastly suffering of the poor and destitute of this district during the famine. It

The eviction of tenants.
(The Illustrated London News, 22-12-1849)

was reported that, 'On every side nothing but cries of death and starvation are heard. The poor are literally dropping on the public highways from hunger.' Similar unforgettable scenes of human misery were also witnessed in the surrounding areas. There were reports of the bodies of women and children lying in ditches along the Dangan and Barna roads. One such casualty was Mark Murphy, who attempted to walk from Spiddal to Galway in January 1848. He was in such a weakened state that death overcame him on the road near Barna. This is the only information available about this unfortunate man.[2]

Patrick and Mary Sweeney and their eleven children made this journey in early September 1849 to secure passage on the brig *St. John*. They were from Lettercallow in Connemara. It is believed that they set out on foot, and if so, it would have been a long and gruelling walk. Their journey to the famine ship would probably have begun about a week before the sailing. The Sweeney family had already survived the worst years of the famine, but with so much hardship behind them they had probably begun to doubt the famine would ever end. Patrick obviously felt that the only future for him and his family lay across the ocean, in America. He hoped to find profitable work in Boston. The fare for the entire family would have left Patrick and Mary with very little money to buy food along the way. Using a little imagination, one can picture the youngest member of the Sweeney family, three-year-old Agnes, hitching a ride on her father's back for at least part of the journey. The beautiful countryside that surrounded them was ravaged by famine and death.

The day after the eviction.
(The Illustrated London News, 16-12-1848)

Village on Mienies, County Cork.
(The Illustrated London News, 20-2-1847)

The Sweeney family's journey to the brig *St. John* took them along the old coast road, through the villages of Spiddal, Barna and Salthill. When they finally arrived in Galway, they found that accommodation was scarce due to the influx of so many other famine refugees. Of course the locals' fear of contracting disease from these refugees added to the scarcity of accommodation.[3]

The Sweeney family avoided the workhouse on Newcastle Road. It had opened in March 1842, and

The Sweeney family home at Lettercallow today.
(Courtesy of John Bhaba Jaick Ó Congaola collection)

was designed to cater for 800 inmates. But by January 1847, 1,143 refugees were being housed there and the number was growing all the time. During the famine, the number of deaths recorded in this establishment each week averaged between twenty-five and thirty. Families were torn apart upon entry to the workhouse, husbands separated from their wives, and children from their parents. For this reason the workhouse was not an option for Patrick and his family; they wished to stay together regardless of the consequences.

As a port town, Galway witnessed a daily influx of poor, destitute and emaciated refugees of all ages. It was only those who had absolutely nothing, were starving and half naked, who made their way to the workhouse. One little six-year-old girl, Celia Griffin from Corandulla, near Ross, arrived in Galway along with her family. All of them were in a 'pitiable condition'. Celia survived for a number of weeks on the streets until she was finally given shelter in the Presentation convent. Although attempts were made to feed her it was too late, and within days her little body finally succumbed to the effects of starvation. Celia was just one of thousands of children who died without understanding why.[4]

In the small parish of Bohermore, where the skipper of the brig *St. John*, Captain Martin Oliver, was living, an average of five people perished every day. A local priest reported that people were so hungry that they had resorted to feeding on nettles and other wild plants. Closer to Galway port, the Claddagh did not escape the clutches of the famine even though it was a fishing village. Cholera struck the Claddagh in 1849, making no distinction between young or old. So many children died that it proved too difficult to record all of their names. The Dominican cemetery book simply kept record of the number of children who died on a particular day.

Spailpín, Brian Connors near Kilrush, County Clare.
(The Illustrated London News, 22-12-1849)

77

The question often asked regarding the famine in the Claddagh, and indeed Connemara, is why did the people not eat fish? It seems that the fish stocks mysteriously disappeared during this period. The herring shoals moved some thirty or forty miles offshore, far beyond the reach of a native currach (a small fishing boat). Another problem was that the sale of fish had traditionally helped pay rent and other debts, while the potato had been the main source of food.[5]

The clergy in Galway were feeding some 4,300 people daily, but were unable to reach everyone. Public relief works included the construction of Threadneedle Road (then called Bóthar na Mine) and the Dyke Road. Those unable to find work, or physically unfit for it, had to find alternative means of feeding themselves and their families, and the number of prisoners in Galway jail soared as a result. Many destitute people sought refuge there by committing petty crime. A fever hospital on Earl's Island, close to the jail, was originally built to accommodate forty patients in four wards, but if necessary could accommodate up to sixty. However, during the famine it became extremely overcrowded. Some of the patients would beg for food on the bridge just outside the grounds, and today it is still known as Beggar's Bridge.

Some people ardently believed that the scarcity of food was created by the British government, who allowed grain and livestock to be exported out of the country during the famine, a view that became widely accepted after the end of the famine. According to one report, the British government spent some seven million pounds on famine relief – a mere five per cent of its gross national profit for that period.

The following poem appeared in the *Galway Mercury* on 10 July 1847:[6]

> 'The Song of the Famine
> (from the University Magazine)'
>
> *Want! want! want!*
> *Under the harvest moon;*
> *Want! want! want!*
> *Thro' dark December's gloom;*
> *To face the fasting day*
> *Upon the frozen flag!*
> *And fasting turn away*
> *To cower beneath a rag.*
>
> *Food! food! food!*
> *Beware before you spurn,*

Ere the cravings of the famishing
To loathing madness turn;
For hunger is a fearful spell,
And fearful work is done,
Where the key to many a reeking crime
Is the curse of living on!

For horrid instincts cleave
Unto the starving life,
And the crumbs they grudge from plenty's feast
But lengthen out the strife –
But lengthen out the pest
Upon the fœtid air,
Alike within the country hut
And the city's crowded lair.

Home! home! home!
A dreary, fireless hole –
A miry floor and a dripping roof,
And a little straw – its whole.
Only the ashes that smoulder not,
Their blaze was long ago,
And the empty space for kettle and pot,
Where once they stood in a row!

Only the naked coffin of deal,
And the little body within,
It cannot shut it out from my sight,
So hunger–bitten and thin;
I hear the small weak moan –
The stare of the hungry eye,
Though my heart was full of a strange, strange joy
The moment I saw it die.

I had food for it e'er yesterday,
But the hard crust came too late;
It lay dry between the dying lips,
And I loathed it – yet I ate.
Three children lie by a cold stark corpse
In the room that's over head –
They have not strength to earn a meal,
Or sense to bury the dead!

And oh! but hunger's a cruel heart,
I shudder at my own,
As I wake my child at a tearless wake,
All lightless and alone!
I think of the grave that waits
And waits but the dawn of day,

And a wish is rife in my weary heart –
I strive and strive, but it won't depart –
I cannot put it away.

Food! food! food!
For the hopeless days begun;
Thank God there's one the less to feel [sic]*!*
I thank God it is my son!
And oh! the dainty winding sheet,
And oh! the shallow grave!
Yet your mother envies you the same
Of all the alms they gave!

Death! death! death!
In lane, and alley, and street,
Each hand is skinny that holds the bier,
And totters each bearer's feet;
The livid faces mock their woe,
And the eyes refuse a tear;
For Famine's gnawing at every heart,
And tramples on love and fear!

Cold! cold! cold!
In the snow, and frost, and sleet,

Cowering over a fireless hearth,
Or perishing in the street.
Under the country hedge,
On the cabin's miry floor,
In hunger, sickness, and nakedness,
It's oh! God help the poor.

It's oh! if the wealthy knew
A tithe of the bitter dole
That coils and coils round the bursting heart
Like a fiend, to tempt the soul!
Hunger, and thirst, and nakedness,
Sorrow, and sickness, and cold,
It's hard to bear when the blood is young,
And hard when the blood is old.

Death! death! death!
Inside of the workhouse bound,
Where maybe a bed to die upon,
And a winding-sheet is found.
For many a corpse lies stiff and stark –
The living not far away –
Without strength to scare the hateful things
That batten upon their prey.

Sick! sick! sick!
With an aching, swimming brain,
And the fierceness of the fever-thirst,
And the maddening famine pain.
On many a happy face
To gaze as it passes by –
To turn from hard and pitiless hearts,
And look up for leave to die.

Food! food! food!
Through splendid street and square,
Food! food! food!
Where is enough and to spare;
And ever so meagre the dole that falls,
What trembling fingers start,
The strongest snatch it away from the weak,
For hunger through walls of stone would break –
It's a devil in the heart!

Like an evil spirit, it haunts my dreams,
Through the silent, fearful night,
Till I start awake from the hideous scenes
I cannot shut from my sight;
They glare on my burning lids,

And thought, like a sleepless goul,
Rides wild on my famine-fevered brain –
Food! ere at last it come in vain
For the body and the soul!

V

PORT OF DEPARTURE
AND HOPE

The new commercial docks in Galway were completed in 1842. The large L-shaped complex gave the town one of the finest harbours on the western seaboard; a harbour that would bear witness to many sad sights following the outbreak of famine. It was from here that the brig *St. John* would sail on its fateful journey a few years later.

As the famine continued many other coffin ships sailed from Galway, carrying with them thousands of poor and destitute people. Among them was *The Barbara* owned by R. D. Persse, *The Wakulla*, *Cushlamachree* and *Alice*. Exactly how many people

Two-Masted Brig.
(Courtesy of Tim Collins)

had sailed from Galway by 1 May 1847 is unknown, but the figure is estimated to be in excess of any full season of emigration in previous years. Some ships also sailed to St Johns, Quebec and New Orleans. Three-quarters of the Irish emigrants setting out on this journey travelled via Liverpool. By 1847, as the situation became increasingly desperate, about one thousand famine refugees were pouring into Liverpool every week. This influx was concentrated within a few

Embarkation at Liverpool Docks.
(The Illustrated London News, 6-7-1850)

square miles of the waterfront. The immigrants were described as 'passive, stunned and mute'. Liverpool's notorious cellars became the popular home for the refugees who did not continue on to America, with as many as forty people at a time sharing a space no more than twelve to fifteen feet wide. A Dr Douglas in Canada stated that one of the main causes of ship fever was the 'filthy slums in which poor emigrants lodged' before embarking on their voyage.[1]

Galway, March 1848.

FOR AMERICA.

For the Flourishing City of BOSTON.

THE SPLENDID NEW BRIG
ALICE
OF GALWAY,
GEORGE M'KAY, Commander,
500 Tons Burthen,

Will Sail for the above Port (wind and weather permitting) on or about the 15th of APRIL next,
And will befitted up in a superior manner for the accommodation of Cabin and Steerage Passengers.

The well-known experience and the proverbial attention of Captain M'KAY to his Passengers renders this vessel a desirable one for Emigrants. The Vessel will be most abundantly supplied with Fuel and Water, and Provisions according to Act of Parliament. Parties would do well to make an early application as a number of berths are already engaged.

For Freight or Passage apply to Bush and Palmer; R. N. Somerville, John Lydon, and Malachy Mannion, Galway; Jas. M'Enerney, Gort; John M'Enerney, Kinvarra; Mr. John Woods, Ballinasloe; Robert Gott, Ballinlough; and Joseph Barrett, Atheury. March 20, 1848.

For the Flourishing City of QUEBEC.

THE SPLENDID NEW SHIP
ABBOTSFORD,
1,000 Tons Burthen, and full Eight Feet between Decks,

Will Sail for the above Port on the 5th of APRIL next (weather permitting). This vessel is only one year old, and the Captain a most experienced man in the Passenger Trade, by whom every attention and kindness will be paid to the Emigrants. The Vessel will be abundantly supplied with Provisions, Fuel and Water, according to act of parliament.

☞ As there are a number of Berths already engaged, early application is necessary to Edmond Duffy, Back-street, or John B. Purdon, Victoria Place, Galway. March 25, 1848.

Advertisements for emigrant ships Alice *and* Abbotsford *out of Galway, March 1848.*
(The Galway Mercury, 25-3-1848)

The brig *St. John* arrived in Galway port during the first week of September 1849. The captain, Martin Oliver, was living in Bohermore at the time, which was only a short distance from the Galway docks. Some sources indicate that Captain Oliver was originally from Scotland. The ship was owned by Henry and Isaac Comerford. One of Henry Comerford's five children, also called Henry, was appointed first mate of the *St. John*. The Comerfords had quite a number of business interests around Galway, including two timber yards, a grain store, a large farm, two offices and a large supply shop where most commodities of the day could be purchased. Henry was married to Margaret, the daughter of Donald McDonagh of Ballykeale House near Kilfenora.

According to *Lloyd's Register of Shipping* of 1845, the *St. John* was built in St John in New Brunswick, Canada, in 1844. This document records the owners as Owens & Company. It was listed as weighing 985 tons but this is incorrect as the ship was actually around 200 tons. The Comerfords purchased the *St. John* from Owens & Company in 1849 at a cost of £1,500. It served as a passenger vessel departing Ireland and as a cargo ship on its return journey. Henry Comerford

PORT OF GALWAY.

ARRIVED FOREIGN.

Verdant, Wallace, Galatz, Indian corn.
Sarah Millidge, M'Donough, Norfolk, Indian flour.

ARRIVED COASTWISE.

Trial, Tick, Clifden, Timber.
Elizabeth, Hunter, London, Indian corn

CLEARED FOREIGN.

Reliance, Bergoyne, Bourdeaux, Ballast.
Bethel, Card, St. John's, passengers.
Warner, Watt, Archangel, Ballast.
Midas, Stitt, St. John's, passengers.

CLEARED COASTWISE.

Newport, Daly, Belmullet, wheat.
Theodore, M'Kay, Ardrossan, ballast.
Julia, Kell, Roundstone, Indian meal.
Maas, Kennedy, London, wheat.

BIRTHS.

At the residence of her father, Henry Comerford, Esq, J.P.
he Lady of Francis Blake Foster, Esq., of a son and heir.
July 8, the lady of Denis Bingham, Esq, of Bingham Cas-
le, county of Mayo, of a daughter.
On the 12th inst., at St. Brandon's, Clonfert, county Galway, the lady of the Rev C. H. Gould Butson, Vicar of Clon-
ert, of a son.

MARRIED

Notice of Henry Cumerfort's ship Sarah Milledge *arriving in
Galway and notice of the birth of his grandson.
(The Galway Mercury, 17-7-1847)*

also owned another ship called the *Sarah Milledge* which he used in the same manner. Other sources state that the brig *St. John* was built and owned by Tony Conneely of Lettermullen in Connemara. These sources indicate that the ship was built at Long Walk in Galway. They also state that Tony Conneely was the first captain and that her maiden voyage took the ship to St John, after which city she was probably named. According to one source the ship was old and well travelled by 1849, having completed many voyages between Ireland and the continent. This would make sense if later reports are correct in stating that the timbers of the overworked ship were rotten and that the old 'hulk' was not seaworthy at the time of the disaster. Nevertheless, it is highly unlikely that the ship was built in Galway given the information recorded in *Lloyd's Register of Shipping*.[2]

Among the crowd assembled at Galway docks on the morning of 7 September 1849 were twenty-seven-year-old Honora (Mary) Burke and her three children. She was pregnant with a fourth child at the time. It is not known why, but her husband remained behind in Galway. Perhaps he was to follow in due course. Twenty-eight-year-old Honora Cullen and her three children were also patiently waiting to board the ship. There is no mention of her husband accompanying her either. Nearby lurked a fourteen-year-old boy, who was trying to camouflage himself amongst the supplies being loaded on to the ship. He did not have the money for his passage and was awaiting an opportunity to slip on board without anyone noticing. The boy had two sisters travelling on the *St. John* and he was determined not to be left behind in Galway. Another passenger, Peggy Mullen, was also preparing to board the ship with her sister's little daughter who she was taking with her on the voyage. The baby's mother had travelled to America on an earlier voyage and was now anxiously awaiting their arrival in Boston. The Egan family, a father, mother and child from Dysart, County Clare, joined the others at the docks. In fact, there was a large gathering from County Clare, with Ennistymon, Lahinch and Kilfenora well represented as can be seen from the passenger list. Natives of Connemara and Galway made up the remainder of the passengers. The thirteen-strong Sweeney family represented the largest family travelling that day. Isaac Comerford, who is listed as one of the sailors and was possibly a son or nephew of the owners, survived the tragedy; he is likely to have been a relative of the owners of the ship.

The two-masted, square-rigged sailing vessel was manned by a crew of sixteen that day. The dockside was crowded with friends and family members bidding tearful goodbyes to their loved ones. Once the ship's supplies had been loaded, approximately one hundred passengers made their way up the gang-plank and located their bunks. The rising tide lifted the 200-ton brig and she was ready to sail. The sailors, supported by the dock crew, cast off and soon the brig was moving out into Galway Bay. There was some excitement among the children as they watched the crew scurrying around the ship and setting the sails in position. The ship rounded Nimmo's Pier and from the main deck the passengers watched as Galway port grew smaller and smaller. The ship sailed past the lighthouse on Mutton Island and on along the coast of Connemara. The poor, unfortunate passengers must have felt that hunger, death and disease were all behind them now and that they were on their way to a better life in America.[3]

According to various sources, the ship anchored

"TEA WATER!"

Tea being served on board an emigrant ship.
(The Illustrated London News, 20-1-1849)

'Soup Time': soup being served on board an emigrant ship.
(The Illustrated London News, 20-1-1849)

off the coast of Lettermullen to take on fresh water supplies, as it was feared that the water in Galway was infected with disease. It is almost certain that a number of additional passengers boarded at Lettermullen. These people were not listed on the ship's manifest and, later, the authorities were later unable to account for all those who had lost their lives. The captain was suspected of pocketing the fares of these new passengers.

Sources indicate that one could obtain a ticket to America by exchanging a bullock to the value of £3. Allegedly, one person from Lettermullen made such an exchange to secure a place on the *St. John*. It was only after the ship had sailed that the true owner of the bullock realised he had been robbed and arrived at the port to reclaim his animal. For most people hard cash was the only currency that secured them a ticket away from hunger.

The ship is believed to have been anchored at Lettermullen for almost a day, and one has to wonder if the *St. John* and its passengers might have outrun the storm had they not delayed for so long. After raising anchor at Lettermullen, the *St. John* sailed out towards the open Atlantic Ocean. The emigrants would have taken one last poignant look at Connemara as it faded from view. While some passengers must have cried for their homeland, knowing they would never see it again, others must have felt cheated by the beautiful but barren land that could no longer sustain its people. What were their thoughts as they sailed out past the Aran Islands?

As the ship ploughed westward, most of the passengers were crammed into narrow compartments below the main deck. Few had been to sea before this sailing and, as on other famine ships, a wave of seasickness would likely have swept over many of the passengers before the Irish coast had even faded from view.[4]

The frightened passengers huddled together in the cramped steerage quarters clutching their rosary beads to their chests as the ship rose and fell with the swell of the ocean. Apart from the threat posed by the unknown watery depths below them, the passengers also feared an outbreak of what was termed 'ship fever', which all too often resulted in death, followed by a lonely burial at sea.

Four days into the journey, the fourteen-year-old-boy was discovered hiding in the hold. His captors were initially very angry and presented him to the

Searching for 'Stowaways'.
(The Illustrated London News, 6-7-1850)

captain, but the issue was soon resolved and the boy was passed into the care of his sisters.

The days of sunshine and clear skies that followed had a calming effect on the passengers. They soon became accustomed to the roll of the sea and found the journey more bearable. At meal times they queued in an orderly fashion to cook their meagre food rations on the small stoves available on the open deck. For women such as Mary Sweeney, who had a husband

and eleven children to take care of, the ship's cooking arrangements can't have made her job easy.

As the weeks passed by, and the coastline of America drew ever closer, there was a growing sense of hope aboard the ship. A fiddler occasionally played some popular tunes that made children scramble to their feet and try their hand at Irish dancing. With the ship making good time under favourable winds, there was a general air of optimism amongst the passengers. As the *St. John* surged forward, its sails billowing in the strong winds, people began to speculate about what the land of hope and promise would bring. During the first week of October the ship entered the waters of the New World and excitement levels reached a crescendo. The passengers knew they were close and they competed for space along the gunwales each day, their eyes scanning the horizon for the first glimpse of the American coastline. They were almost there. Memories of their homeland, where hunger stalked every road and boreen, began to fade away. The following poem, which was published in the *Galway Mercury* on 5 September 1846, describes the hardship the passengers had left behind:[5]

'Song of the Famine
(From the Fireman)'

Knee deep in the furrow
The peasant stands,
And he wringeth in sorrow
His toil-worn hands;
And wan and woe smitten
His forehead – for care
And famine have written
His misery there.

He hath delved and upturned
Of his garden a rood,
Where blighted and burned
Lies his rot-stricken food;
The earth he had riven,
Its rottenness baring –
He looketh to Heaven,
Heartbroken, despairing.

Now enter his cottage.
Where starving in common,
Lie shivering dotage

And suffering women;
Yet, pause if you cower –
By contagion are scared;
Here fevers devour
What famine hath spared.

For drink hoarsely craving
On the damp ground reclining,
See writhing and raving
In the pestilence pining,
'Til death, hailed with pleasure,
Blackened corpses, now strews 'em
His child – his heart's treasure –
And the wife of his bosom.

Oh, God, in deep mystery
Thy Providence veiling
The peasants' sad history,
Shall it waken no feeling? –
Shall our land be by famine
And pestilence trod?
Deus vetat – *oh, amen!*
Forbid it, oh, God!

VI

TRAGEDY ON
GRAMPUS ROCK

On Saturday, 6 October 1849, the brig *St. John* entered
the waters of Boston Harbour. It had been a good
voyage; faster and less hazardous than people had
expected for that time of year. The captain gave orders
that a ration of 'ardent spirits' be issued to the crew
and suggested that the passengers should celebrate
their last night on board the *St. John*. The rigging and
deck were decorated with candles and plans to spend
the night in song and dance were put in place. They
had good reason to celebrate for they had left a land of
starvation, disease and death behind them, and ahead
lay a land fertile with hope.

Dancing between the decks.
(The Illustrated London News, 6-7-1850)

It was late afternoon. A light rain began to fall on the passengers as they watched the American coastline draw nearer. At around 5 p.m. the ship passed the Cape Cod Lighthouse. The rain may have dampened their bodies but not their spirits, as their new home beckoned just a short distance away. The rain continued to fall, becoming heavier as the evening wore on, and eventually driving the people below deck. The passengers tried to console one another, saying that within a few hours their journey would be complete and the dangers of the sea would be behind them. However, the sailors' pale faces betrayed their fear. The weather continued to deteriorate and by midnight a gale was blowing from the north-east. Howling winds and giant waves crashed against the ship with all their might. The terrified passengers huddled together and listened as the brig's groaning timbers struggled to withstand the force of such powerful elements.[1]

The captain gave orders to his crew to lay a course north-east in an attempt to escape the wraith of the storm. Throughout the late evening and night large waves and strong winds continued to pummel the brig. Sometime after midnight, the attack took its toll and the ship's timbers began to loosen. There was no reprieve for the *St. John*. Directly ahead of the ship lay the rocks of Marblehead, jutting out ominously like the exposed teeth of a predator. A similar threat awaited the ship at Graves Ledge. Even the howling storm could not drown out the terrified cries of the passengers below deck; the sinister groans of the brig's hull further unnerving them.

By 1 a.m. on 7 October the fierce winds had driven the ship southwards along Massachusetts Bay. At around 4 a.m. Captain Martin realised that it would be impossible to out-sail the storm and he ordered his crew to change course and head towards the southern shores of Massachusetts Bay. But the huge waves and strong winds forced the brig towards the Cohasset coastline instead. As dawn broke, the captain stared out through the mist of rain and wind and saw Minot's Ledge in the distance, an area well known for shipwrecks. Nearby, he could see huge white waves smashing against the deadly rocks of Grampus Ledge. Both he and the other experienced sailors knew that they were in grave trouble and that their courage and leadership was about to be tested to the extreme.[2]

As the skies brightened another brig, the *Kathleen*, could be seen from the deck of the *St. John*. She lay just inside the breakers at Hocksett Rock, close to Cohasset harbour, and was also caught in the violent grip of the storm. Her sails had been torn to shreds by the storm and she had dropped anchor, but was still being dragged. On board the *St. John*, Captain Oliver

Opposite page: Map of the Cohasset and Scituate Harbours

quickly assessed the situation and realised that the *Kathleen* was no longer in danger. Although the ship had taken a ferocious beating, she was no longer on course to collide with the granite ledges and at worse she would run aground on the sandy Cohasset shore.

From his deck Captain Oliver could see roaring white plumes of foam shooting high into the air and crashing back down against Grampus Ledge. He knew that unless his ship could evade these treacherous rocks, they were doomed. Although the sails had already been lowered, the bare masts were swaying dangerously in the violent winds. The captain had no way of steering the brig effectively so he ordered his crew to drop anchor. There was a rattle of chains and moments later the anchors sunk into the sea bed; there was a shudder, as the ship was held in place.[3] Captain Oliver hoped and prayed that the anchors would hold the *St. John* in position until the storm abated. It was a desperate gamble. However, his hope was short-lived as before long the anchors began to drag. Mountainous waves were now battering the hull and it became impossible to hold the ship in position. Each wave drew the *St. John* closer to the treacherous rocks of Grampus Ledge. Below deck the terrified passengers had begun praying. The Act of Contrition, amongst other prayers, was being offered up to God in a desperate plea for mercy. Several passengers had made their way onto the main deck and, terror-stricken, they huddled together as the ship lunged towards the granite face of Grampus Ledge.

In a last desperate bid for survival, Captain Oliver shouted at his crew to cut the masts, praying that this might lessen the impact of the ferocious winds. The masts and their rigging were promptly cut but it was too late. The breakers now measured between twenty and thirty feet in height and each one brought the ship ever closer to Grampus Ledge. Finally, the ocean seeming to have grown tired of toying with its prey, one last enormous wave sealed the fate of the ship and sent her smashing into the rocks of Grampus Ledge. The initial impact punched a huge gaping hole in the hull and many of the passengers below deck were drowned immediately. The *St. John* was smashed against the rocks repeatedly. The weakened timbers finally succumbed to the power of the sea and the ship began to come apart at the seams as the people on board cried out to heaven for mercy.[4]

The passengers and crew clambered towards the

Boston Harbour circa 1850s.
(Courtesy of John Bhaba Jaick Ó Congaola collection)

ship's jolly-boat and longboat. Men, women and children clung to the gunwales as the merciless waves crashed down upon them. The waves snatched many from the heaving deck and delivered them to the hungry sea. Alongside the hull, the ship's jolly-boat was swaying from its tackles. Suddenly the stern rigging bolt snapped and the boat plummeted into the sea. One of the tackles held and the jolly-boat stayed afloat.

Captain Oliver realised that if he could clear the line, he might be in a position to get some of the passengers and crew into the boat. Along with his second mate, two members of his crew and two apprentice boys, the captain managed to jump into the jolly-boat even though it was rocking wildly in the stormy sea. When the passengers spotted the captain and his crew seated in the small jolly-boat, a fresh wave of panic swept over them and they flung themselves at their one chance of survival. Some twenty-five passengers swamped the tiny vessel and it instantly began to sink. Almost all those on board the jolly-boat perished. Only Captain Oliver and one other man managed to battle against the waves long enough to be hauled back on board the sinking brig. Some sources indicate that Captain Oliver was the only survivor of the jolly-boat. He is said to have grabbed a rope hanging from the quarter deck and was rescued from the water by his first mate, Henry Comerford.[5]

The longboat was now the only possibility of salvation, but it had broken loose from the brig and each wave carried it further and further away from the sinking ship. It was certain death for anyone who remained aboard the sinking vessel, so the passengers and crew began flinging themselves at the mercy of the sea, intending to swim towards the longboat. Only twelve made it: the captain, the first mate, eight other crew members and two passengers. One of the passengers to clamber aboard the longboat was the boy who had stowed away on the brig; his sisters were drowned. Amongst those swept overboard were Mary Sweeney and her remaining children, as several of them had already been drowned when the ship first hit the rocks. As the *St. John* was breaking up, Mary's husband Patrick grabbed their youngest child, three-year-old Agnes, and climbed down one of the ropes hanging from the doomed ship. Clutching his little girl he struck out for the longboat. Tragically, moments later father and child were struck by a powerful wave and the last two members of the Sweeney family perished together. Their fate was shared by the majority of the emigrants. Peggy Mullen and her sister's baby were lost to the sea, as were the Egan family from County Clare, Honora (Mary) Burke's three children and all of Honora Cullen's children.

When the brig finally split in two the remaining passengers were swept into the sea, where they thrashed about wildly, trying to grab on to any debris to stay afloat. A large section of the brig's deck had split from the ship and it saved the lives of seven men and two women. They held onto this piece of wreckage and were washed ashore on the Cohasset beach some time later.[6] The majority of the other passengers were not so lucky. The coastline lay less than a mile from the ill-fated ship, but most of the passengers would never make it onto American soil.

VII

COHASSET SHOCKED

The people of Cohasset had been watching the disaster unfold from the windows of their homes since dawn. At first all they could do was offer up prayers for those on board the stricken vessel. One such onlooker was nineteen-year-old Elizabeth Lothrop. It was about eight o'clock in the morning when she noticed the two ships about a mile offshore. She informed her father, Captain John Jacob Lothrop Jr, a seafarer. He immediately recognised the danger the ships were in and went to assist the Humane Society volunteer lifeboat crew who were preparing to put to sea. Meanwhile, Elizabeth made her way to beach accompanied by her brothers.

By now a small crowd of locals had gathered on the beach to stare out through the driving rain and wind at the troubled ships. They could see that the *Kathleen* was closer to the shore and away from the dangerous rocks. Suddenly one of the locals pointed towards a rogue wave of enormous proportions that was rising up from the sea. Within seconds a fifty-foot wall of green water, topped by a froth of angry white foam, was bearing down on the mastless *St. John* and its terrified human cargo. It crashed down upon the *St. John* with an angry roar, flinging the vessel against the rocks with such force that it looked like a toy boat in the hands of a reckless child. The *St. John*'s hull snapped like a twig as twenty-foot waves pounded her relentlessly, each one sweeping more men, women and children out to sea. Some of the Cohasset onlookers were convinced that they could hear the victims' screams above the howling winds and the raging sea. Many of the locals would normally have shown little concern for Irish immigrants, but they were overcome with emotion as the tragedy unfolded before them.[1]

The volunteer lifeboat crew put to sea at Whitehead near Cohasset Harbour. They rowed as fast as they could against the enormous waves. A second lifeboat also set out and an express message was sent to Boston to enlist the help of the *R.B. Forbes*, but this vessel was already in use on another mission. Despite a tremendous effort, the second, smaller lifeboat and its seven-man crew were unable to reach the sinking ship and were forced to return to shore. After some forty-five minutes the first lifeboat reached the longboat, which was carrying Captain Oliver and several others, as they pulled for the shore. The lifeboat crew could see that the brig was now almost underwater and, believing that the *St. John*'s only survivors were in the lifeboat, they turned their attentions towards guiding the *Kathleen* ashore. It seems that the passengers of the longboat made no attempt to inform the lifeboat crew that there were people still afloat close to the *St. John* wreck. The lifeboat was capable of carrying twenty people, and it is unknown how many passengers were still afloat at this time. But the lifeboat crew, deafened by the wind and blinded by sheets of rain and sea spray, had no idea that there were still survivors in the water. As the lifeboat steered away from the *St. John*, the fate of the passengers still desperately clinging to pieces of wreckage was sealed. The crew of the lifeboat rowed in the direction of the *Kathleen*, which was now sending out distress signals. They reached the troubled ship in good time. The captain, fearing that his ship was not yet out of danger, requested that the lifeboat crew take on board five children. The lifeboat then guided the *Kathleen* to safety.[2]

Elizabeth Lothrop recorded the following account in her diary a few days after the *St. John* sank. She first observed the disaster from the window of her home and then she joined her brothers on the beach Elizabeth mentions that a whaling boat was in the vicinity of the *St. John* when it sank; however, this was not recorded in any other document that was researched for this book:

> *I arrived home a week ago last Tuesday and I have had such unpleasant weather I have not had an opportunity to look about me. Then last Sunday my eyes were opened in the following manner: About eight o'clock I made a visit to the sea room for something, where I heard an exclamation from one of the boys, which drew my attention on the sea, where I saw two brigs, one anchored in the midst of rocks with the sea breaking upon her from all sides, the other further off and apparently out of danger. I*

went below and informed father, he looked out and said 'there is difficulty there'. Soon her masts were cut away. Father had gone to join the lifeboat, my brothers all for the beach, I noticed she drifted in rapidly, and if her anchors could not hold her she would inevitably soon be on the rocks where the waves were fast forcing her with horrible vengeance, no human power could stay those waves, their aim was destruction, and how forcibly it was carried into execution was soon declared to my horror-stricken vision. In about an hour after her masts were cut away nothing was visible, in a moment she had gone to atoms and the sea had washed over the fragments, freighted with human beings. Soon, portions of the brig could be seen making for the shore now towering up mountains high and then sinking into the depths of hell. Whether there were human beings on board the wreck the thickness of the storm prevented me from determining then.

Soon the multitudes with which the beach was thronged began to wave their hats and halloo, and I understood afterwards that when they observed people on the wreck, it was a motion for a whale boat to come alongside which paid no heed to the demand, which was one of the many inhuman actions of the day, which displayed such perfect indifference to human suffering, such unaccountable hardness of heart that thinks of nothing but self ease and protection. The waving of hats led me to infer there were human beings on board the wreck. I forthwith began to put things in readiness, heat rooms and blankets, make beds, as ours is the nearest house the sufferers would all be brought in for relief.[3]

The passengers aboard the longboat rowed with all their might against the stormy sea, almost capsizing several times. Over an hour later they reached the safety of the beach, where anxious locals swarmed around them and wrapped them in blankets. They were then given shelter at a summer boarding house near Sandy Cove, which was run by the Lothrop and Whittington families. The house had already been prepared for the survivors and contained a plentiful supply of clean sheets, blankets, etc.

A handful of passengers who had managed to hold onto the floating debris of the *St. John* were washed ashore some time later. Their hands had to be pried away from the planks of timber that had saved their lives. One man found himself carried towards the rocks on board a piece of wreckage that he refused to part with. A rescuer had to jump onto the small piece of debris, fasten a rope around the man and pull him to safety. Upon reaching the beach the man's face was described as being a 'deep purple', induced by a combination of terror and cold. His mouth gaped open and his 'fixed teeth, and deathly eyes, formed a sight long to be remembered'.

The iron-tight grasp with which the survivors had clung to the wreckage was transferred to the clothing of their rescuers. Even after reaching the shelter and safety of the boarding house many of them found it difficult to let go.

Two of the women who made it ashore were Honora (Mary) Burke and Honora Cullen. Both women had lost their children. One can only imagine the horror and anguish they must have experienced when they realised their children were lost to them forever. It is likely that they also felt a measure of guilt at having survived when their children had not been so lucky. Their heartbroken moans could be heard by the other survivors all through the day and the night that followed.

Doctor Foster from the village of Cohasset tended

to the survivors and did his utmost to ensure their comfort. One survivor, referred to only as Mrs Quinlan, and who was not recorded on the passenger list of the *St. John*, was taken to the Cohasset almshouse, along with Honora (Mary) Burke, for more intensive medical treatment. Honora (Mary) Burke, who was pregnant at the time, later recovered, but it is not known whether her baby survived.

Elizabeth Lothrop was at the shelter to offer her support when the survivors arrived and she later recorded the following entry in her diary:

I had enough to do, with an occasional glance out the window when at last I perceived some miserable looking creatures, that reminded me of drowned rats approaching. They could scarcely walk and were led by men on either side of them, our doors were open to receive them. Such a shuddering shivering my ears never heard before, and such a set of half drowned half naked half frightened creatures my eyes never beheld.

Three men were first brought in and then a lot of women, all Irish. What conclusion to make I did not [know;] *if it were not for the exigency of*

*the moment, we should have been overpowered by
excitement. We placed them in bed, and used every
exertion to restore animation to two of the women
whose moans could be heard through the house. These
two were senseless when taken from the wreck,
towards night six were able to go to the village in a
week the worst were conveyed to the poor house.*

Shortly after the survivors reached safety, the bodies
of the victims began washing up along the beach. The
locals covered them with blankets while they waited
for the delivery of coffins that were being hastily
assembled by local carpenters. Many of the bodies had
been badly mutilated by the jagged rocks. However,
the body of one of the victims, that of Sally Sweeney,
was unscathed; her features were described as looking
'calm and placid as if she were enjoying a quiet and
pleasant slumber'. Some of the bodies had been flung
onto the rocks closer to shore and were now being
swept away by the retreating sea. A man by the name
of Charles Studley made a brave attempt to retrieve
one such body, but he nearly drowned in the process
and had to be rescued.[4]

Another man, a Mr Holmes, was said to have spent

the day tending to the survivors and trying to rescue bodies from the surf.

At some point during the day, while walking along the shoreline, Captain Lothrop spotted a parcel of clothing bobbing up and down in the surf. He waded into the water and retrieved the parcel. Upon opening it, he discovered to his absolute delight an infant alive and well. It was reported some days later that the baby was in perfect health, and had been entrusted into the temporary care of the Gove family from the village.[5]

Urgent messages had been sent to Boston to inform the authorities of the tragic news, and the following day handbills were circulated on the streets proclaiming, 'Death! One hundred and forty-five lives lost at Cohasset.' The terrible news spread quickly and stunned everyone, particularly the small Irish communities of Fort Hill and South Cove. The residents of some of these communities had been awaiting the arrival of family members on the *St. John*. They made further enquiries of the fate of the ship's passengers, hoping for good news, but fearing the worst. They gathered together at meetings in the homes of friends and neighbours, where it was decided that they would go to Cohasset and offer their assistance.[6]

VIII

RECOVERY AND BURIAL

On Tuesday morning members of Boston's Irish community began arriving in Cohasset. It was only then that the full enormity of the tragedy was revealed to them. For many their worst fears were well founded and their loved ones were dead. Local people were already combing the beaches looking for bodies and the devastated families joined in the search. Fragments of the wreckage of the *St. John*, that included hats, bonnets, dresses, scarves and jackets, were spread across the shoreline. Breakers were still crashing angrily against the rocks and washing over a small section of the *St. John* that still remained afloat. A reporter from the *Boston Daily Herald* arrived in Cohasset during the day and gave the following brief account of what he witnessed in the wake of the tragedy:

> *One of our reporters visited the scene of the lament–*
> *able catastrophe yesterday, and states that the sight*
> *was heart-rending in the extreme. The shore, for*
> *about a mile in length, was strewed with portions*
> *of the wreck. Some of the bodies were shockingly*
> *mutilated. The forehead of one the woman* [sic]
> *was horribly mangled; the flesh from the right leg*
> *of another was torn off from above the knee to the*
> *feet; all the others were more or less bruised, with*
> *the exception of one young girl, recognised as Sally*
> *Sweeny* [sic], *whose person exhibited no injuries.*[1]

Henry David Thoreau, an American writer, and his friend Ellery Channing, a poet, arrived in Boston in the aftermath of the tragedy. They had planned to meet the Provincetown steamer, which should have docked the previous day, but had not arrived because of the storm. Thoreau noticed a handbill announcing the terrible news and he and his companion decided to go to Cohasset to investigate the reports. He later documented the tragic event in his book, *Cape Cod.*

He recorded that along the way he met many Irish people travelling to Cohasset to identify the bodies and help tend to the survivors. They were also on their way to the funerals, the first of which was supposed to take place that afternoon. It appeared that all of the people travelling to Cohasset that morning were bound for the beach. People were also flocking in from the neighbouring county. Hundreds of people arrived on foot or in wagons. Among them were sportsmen still dressed in hunting jackets, carrying guns and game bags, and flanked by dogs. On the way to the beach, Thoreau and Channing passed Cohasset General Cemetery where they noted that a hole as deep and large as a cellar had been freshly dug. A winding, rocky road led to the shore, along which several hay-riggings and farm wagons were returning, each carrying three large coffins. The owners of the wagons were acting as temporary undertakers. Nearer the shore horses and carriages were secured to the fences. People dotted the beach for a mile or so in either direction, searching for bodies and examining the washed-up fragments of the wreck.[2]

Thoreau and Channing arrived in Cohasset two days after the storm yet the waves were still breaking violently on the rocks. Thoreau observed a collection of coffins lying on a green hillside a short distance from the water. A small crowd had gathered around these boxes. About twenty-seven or twenty-eight bodies had been recovered. Items of clothing that could only be described as rags were still attached to the bodies, but they were now being covered with white sheets and placed in the coffins. Irish relatives were trying to lift the lids to identify the bodies of their friends and family.

Some of the men involved in the grim task of preparing the bodies for burial were rapidly nailing down the coffin lids. According to Thoreau, these men carried out their work with a 'sober dispatch of business'. In some cases two or more children, or a parent and child, were placed in the same coffin. Once a body had been identified, the name was recorded in red chalk on the lid of the coffin.

At this point the bodies of Peggy Mullen and her sister's child had been recovered and had been placed in the same coffin. Peggy's sister, who had travelled to America on an earlier ship, had been anxiously awaiting the arrival of her baby and her sister when news of the tragedy spread through the streets of Boston. With great apprehension she made her way along the rocky road that led to Cohasset beach. She spent some time walking along the shore, seeking information on her child or sister, but no one could tell her anything. Finally, her heart beating wildly in her chest, she made her way towards the bodies. There, to her horror, she discovered her sister still alive but lying in a coffin with her arms wrapped around her little baby girl. The broken-hearted mother died three days later, adding one more victim to the tragedy's death toll.

When the bodies had all been assigned a coffin, they were placed on the wagons to await removal. Henry Thoreau gave the following graphic description of the harrowing scenes he witnessed:

> *I saw many marble feet and matted heads as the cloths were raised, and one livid, swollen, and mangled body of a drowned girl – who probably had intended to go out to service in some American family – to which some rags still adhered, with a string, half concealed by the flesh, about its swollen neck; the coiled-up wreck of human a hulk, gashed by the rocks or fishes, so that the bone and muscle were exposed, but quite bloodless – merely red and white*

— with wide-open and staring eyes, yet lustreless,
dead-lights; or like the cabin windows of a stranded
vessel, filled with sand.[3]

Thoreau and Channing walked further along the rocky
shore. In the first cove they came upon they found
what appeared to be fragments of the brig strewn
about the place and mixed up with sand, seaweed and
large quantities of feathers. The wreckage was in such
bad condition that at first Thoreau believed the timbers
to belong to an old wreck that had most likely lain
there for many years. Thoreau asked a nearby sailor if
this was indeed the wreckage of the *St. John*. The sailor
replied that it was. Thoreau then asked him where the
ship had struck the rocks and the sailor pointed to
Grampus Rock which lay about a mile from shore.

'You can see a part of her now sticking up; it looks
like a small boat,' the sailor added.

Thoreau then enquired if the bodies he had seen
earlier represented all of the victims.

'Not a quarter of them,' replied the sailor.

'Where are the rest?'

'Most of them right underneath that piece you
see.'

There was a sufficient amount of debris scattered along the shore to make people think that this represented the whole of the wreckage but it would take several days for it to be uncovered and removed in its entirety.

Among the crowd gathered on the shore were local men, busy gathering clumps of seaweed that had washed ashore during the storm. They were moving this valuable manure beyond the reach of the tide so that it could later be loaded onto carts and taken away for use on their land. Thoreau recorded that although they were often obliged to separate fragments of clothing from the seaweed, and might at any moment have exposed a body, they still seemed unwilling to let this seaweed go to waste. [4]

As Thoreau and his companion continued along the beach, poignant indicators of the extent of the tragedy caught their attention: a man's clothing had snagged on some rocks, and a woman's scarf, a gown and a straw bonnet had washed ashore. They also encountered one of the *St. John*'s masts which had been broken into several pieces. In stark contrast to this scene, about a mile to the south the masts of the *Kathleen* could be seen, now safely docked in Cohasset harbour.

In another rocky cove along the water's edge lay an intact section of one side of the *St. John*'s hull. It was almost completely hidden away behind rocks, some of which were about twenty feet high. The wreckage was perhaps forty feet long by fourteen feet wide. The powerful waves had left their mark on this section of the hull; even the largest pieces of timbers and iron braces hadn't managed to withstand their destructive power. Thoreau noted that some parts of the timber were so rotten that he could almost pierce them with his umbrella. He was later surprised to learn that some of the survivors had come ashore clinging to this decayed section of the ship.[5]

A little further along the beach Thoreau and his companion came across a number of men crowded around the first mate of the *St. John*, who was giving his account of the tragedy. He spoke of the captain as the master of the ship and seemed a little excited as he gave his account of the disaster. Obviously speaking of the jolly-boat, he was saying that when they jumped into the boat it filled with water which caused the 'painter' to break and sink. Another sailor stood on a rock close by, he was chewing tobacco and gazing out at the sea. He turned and called to his companion, saying, 'Let's be off. We've seen the whole of it. It's no use to stay to the funeral.' Continuing along the shoreline, Thoreau and Channing encountered one of the male survivors of the brig. Thoreau described him as a 'sober-looking man, dressed in a jacket and gray pantaloons, with his hands in the pockets'. Thoreau asked him a few questions, which he answered, but he seemed reluctant to talk about his ordeal and after a few moments he walked away. One of the lifeboat men had been standing by his side, dressed in an oil-cloth jacket. He told Thoreau and his companion how he and the lifeboat crew had gone to the aid of the *Kathleen*, thinking that all the survivors from the *St. John* had been in the longboat and were safely deposited on the beach. The huge waves had prevented the lifeboat crew from seeing the passengers still afloat beside the sinking vessel.

Having spoken with the lifeboat man, Thoreau and Channing moved further up the beach and found the flag of the *St. John* spread on a rock, as if it had been left there to dry. They continued their walk as far as a headland called Whitehead. There, in a little cove, they met an old man and his son collecting seaweed, their expressions placid, as though they had no knowledge of the tragedy that had befallen so many innocent people only two days earlier. When questioned, the old man said that he had heard about the wreck and knew most of the particulars, but had not been to the area since it happened. His main concern was the various weeds he carried in his arms – rock-weed, kelp and seaweed.[6]

The first set of funerals took place in the afternoon on Tuesday 9 October. The religious services were performed by Revd Reid and Revd Joseph Osgood, both Unitarian ministers in Cohasset. The services were held in the local church. However, before the remains of the victims were removed for burial a question arose over the type of service that should be held at the graveside. It was decided that because the victims were predominantly Catholic, and it being the wish of the relatives, a priest would perform the graveside ceremony. Fr John T. Roddan from Quincy was asked to carry out the service. A common grave was dug on the highest point of Cohasset General Cemetery, with a commanding view of the bay. The mass grave measured over twenty feet long, and was nine feet wide and six feet deep. After the church service, the funeral procession took place, with Captain Oliver and the survivors of the *St. John* leading the way. As the funeral party neared the cemetery, hundreds of people were still arriving in Cohasset. The *Boston Daily Herald* later reported that as the coffins were being covered a number of horse-cars arrived from Boston. Among the passengers was the sister of Miss Peggy Adams, one of the victims. Her husband accompanied her. They had come from South Boston and wished to view the body of Miss Adams. The coffin containing the remains was opened at her request. The woman experienced a most 'poignant agony' upon seeing the body of her sister. The sight of this 'melancholy reunion' touched all those present. Peggy Adams was not recorded among the *St. John*'s passengers.[7]

IX

THE AFTERMATH

Over the following days a constant vigil of the shoreline was maintained in the hope of recovering more bodies. Numerous bodies were still drifting off-shore and over time many of them were recovered. During the following weeks forty-five bodies in total were buried in the mass grave. These burials must have been spread out over a number of days or indeed weeks, with a section of the mass grave being left open to allow for the addition of new bodies. While some sources state that none of the forty-five bodies were identified, this cannot be true given Henry Thoreau's eyewitness account in which he mentions the names of some of the victims being recorded in red chalk on the lids of their coffins. The fact that the coffins were opened to allow the survivors to view their relatives would also indicate that some of the victims were identified.

On 4 November 1849, almost a month after the disaster, Fr Roddan returned to Cohasset to celebrate the first Catholic mass to be held in the town. It took place in the local high school hall and was attended by Irish and Portuguese fishermen and their families who were living in the area at the time. The mass was sponsored by relatives of the *St. John* survivors and was dedicated to the memory of the victims. Mass has continued to be held in Cohasset every year since the catastrophe to commemorate all those who lost their lives.

Over the years many ships had been lost in the dangerous waters of Cohasset Bay but the tragedy of the brig *St. John* was the worst to befall the area. In 1847 plans for a lighthouse for Minot's Ledge had been drawn up in an effort to prevent tragedies but it was New Year's Day 1850 before its light finally shone down on the bay. However, the lighthouse proved unstable and in 1860 it was replaced by a new structure that took five years to complete. A lady from Cohasset, Mary Barnes, later wrote the following lines of poetry in commemoration of the tragedy:[1]

What think ye, as ye stand there where rises this
shaft of stone?
The dreams and hopes of fellow men facing the land
of light.
What think ye, oh Spirit Survivor as ye stand there
all alone?

Elizabeth Lothrop was later sent a sum of $10 by the L.T. (benevolent) Society for the kindness she showed the survivors. She returned the money, saying that 'it might be better employed' elsewhere. In the days following the disaster, she confided in her diary that so great was the tragedy's effect on her that she feared her life would never be the same again. She would never be as 'happy and carefree' as she had been before that dreadful day. She wrote of a profound sadness that never seemed to abate. The following extracts from her diary indicate how the tragedy affected her. They also reveal that the bodies of the brig's victims continued to wash ashore for some time after the disaster:

I attended church today after a long absence, but my mind is so full of everything, I cannot pay much attention to the disclosures. A dancing school has commenced I do not attend it but my mind runs the way; then this horrible shipwreck, and the continual picking up of dead bodies on our beach, has so excited my mind that I tell them I shall never get over it.

I took a walk on the beach after meeting, and there I saw two or three bodies stretched out. I did not approach very near to them, as I was told, they looked like anything but human beings. Last Wednesday I called at the poor house to see those two who were taken from here a day or two previous. Mrs Quinlan and Mrs Burke, I found they had improved rapidly. I should judge they had good care taken of them. I found but twelve paupers in the poor house, and some curious looking objects ...[2]

A week after the tragedy Captain Oliver and his first mate were called before the local authorities to give their accounts of what had happened. Captain Oliver stated that his ship had passed 'Cape Cod Light at about 5 p.m. on Saturday' and reached 'Scituate Light at 1.00 a.m. on Sunday'. He told them that he had 'stood northward for about three hours to clear land. As daylight approached, he tacked the ship and stood South, South, West. The weather was very thick.'

Coming inside of Minot's Ledge, he caught sight of another brig anchored inside the breakers. At Hocksett Rock he had tried to 'wear away up to the brig, but found he could not fetch up'. He dropped both anchors in the hope of holding the ship in position and avoiding a collision with the rocks. Captain Oliver informed the inquiry that the anchors had dragged. He recalled instructing his crew to cut the masts away but the ship had continued to drift and was eventually forced onto Grampus Ledge and destroyed. The authorities did not hold Captain Oliver accountable for the tragedy. However, a report from the *Galway Vindicator* argued that the captain should have been held accountable for at least some of his actions:

> *From further conversation with the passengers and people of the town, it is certain to mind that Captain Oliver is liable to severe censure for some parts of his conduct. We would be the last to say one word that would add to the poignancy of his feelings in view of his great disaster; but, in a question involving the lives of more than one hundred fellow beings, we are bound to speak faithfully, the truth, as it has been presented to us.*

It seems that on the afternoon of Saturday 6th inst., he numbered his passengers. Upwards of one hundred names were borne upon the manifest, or list, as two passengers called it who answered to the call. A line was then drawn across the deck, and between twenty and thirty other names were borne upon a small memorandum book. If the consignee has a duplicate list of passengers he or they should produce it. Unless a complete list can be produced we can never fully ascertain the exact number who perished on board this vessel on the fatal morning of October 9 [sic].[3]

On 1 January 1979, the curator of the Maritime Museum in Cohasset recorded further criticism of Captain Oliver's actions. He stated in a letter that when the Cohasset lifeboat encountered Captain Oliver in the *St. John* longboat, the captain allegedly shouted, in reference to the wreckage, 'Don't bother wasting your time. There is no one left alive.' However, shortly after the disaster Captain Lothrop gave a written statement that said that on approaching the longboat neither Captain Oliver nor his crew showed 'any intention of communicating with us which they might easily have done being directly to windward of us'. A degree of doubt exists as to whether Captain Lothrop was in fact on board the lifeboat, but this first-hand statement strongly indicates that he was. In any case, both of these statements are damning insofar as Captain Oliver either gave his rescuers incorrect information or none at all.

The crew of the lifeboat were later astonished to discover that there had been so many fatalities. Had they known that survivors were still clinging onto the wreckage of the *St. John* they could have tried to rescue them as they were closer to the brig than to the *Kathleen* at the time. Regardless of what Captain Oliver did or did not say to his rescuers, he must undoubtedly have had a difficult time trying to explain to the authorities how it was that he and so many of his crew had survived when so many passengers had died. Little is known of what happened to Captain Oliver following the disaster. Some say that he went out west and simply disappeared. There are also some conflicting records that do not list Martin as his Christian name. However, the majority of sources state that his name was Martin Oliver.

Reports indicate that the *St. John* was an 'aging and

somewhat unseaworthy craft' at the time of its fatal voyage. It was also noted that the timbers were 'rotten'. However, the owners of the ship do not seem to have commented on its tragic end and its questionable state of repair, though it is possible that their reaction was simply not recorded. Both Henry and Isaac Comerford later became justices of the peace in Galway. Henry Comerford died on 6 September 1861 at Ballykeale House in his sixty-seventh year. According to one source, three of *St. John*'s cabin passengers were nieces of Henry Comerford. With the exception of the Sweeney family, the only other three sisters recorded among the victims are Honora, Mary and Margaret Mulkenan, but they were listed as steerage passengers. Nevertheless, it is my opinion that these three sisters were the nieces of Henry Comerford.[4]

All of the survivors of the *St. John* eventually returned to Ireland, with the exception of one woman, Mary Kane Cole, who settled in Cohasset. In 1868 she married a local man. Ironically, his name was James St John. Twenty-four-year-old Mary was already a widow when she sailed to America on the *St. John*. Her husband, Charles Cole, had died in Ireland and Mary had boarded the ship in the hope of starting life anew in America. James St John was a tailor and store-keeper in America. A father of five children, James had also been widowed. James and Mary had no children of their own. Mary died in 1917.

According to local sources in Lettermullen, some of the *St. John* survivors, who had not been recorded on the ship's manifest, also returned home. They included Martin and Patrick Flaherty, who were brothers, and a second Patrick Flaherty, who was seemingly not related. One of the sailors who survived was James Flaherty, also from Lettermullen. Today, descendants of these survivors still live in the Lettermullen area. The baby girl rescued from the sea by Captain Lothrop was adopted by a family named Norwell. She later married into an Irish immigrant family from Boston. They became wealthy land dealers in the Dorchester Bay area. This baby was not included on the original list of survivors.[5]

In the aftermath of the tragedy, rumours surfaced of certain individuals profiting from the ship sinking; all of these rumours are unfounded. In 1984 a newspaper published an account, or more correctly a rumour, that accused the captain of trying to flee west with the passengers' gold, which had been hidden in a wooden box or chest which the newspaper identified as 'the captain's strong box'. This is highly unlikely considering that the captain would have been preoccupied with saving his own life when escaping from the doomed ship. It is also highly unlikely that his passengers would have possessed nearly enough gold to fill such a box. These poor, unfortunate, starving people were fleeing from famine and had hardly enough money to feed themselves.

Another account indicates that the chest was actually owned by one of the survivors. He supposedly left it at the Lothrop house in Sandy Cove after he had recovered from his ordeal and moved away. However, there is yet another story concerning the captain's strong box to consider. In an undated letter, a local woman named Lucy Treat writes that her father had once told her of a strange scene he came upon the day after the *St. John* tragedy. He had been walking along the beach when he encountered a neighbour hauling a chest after him. The neighbour hid this chest near Sandy Cove. Shortly afterwards this man was said to have become 'conspicuous by his ability to afford unusual luxuries and also paid off a mortgage on his house within the year'. According to the letter, two generations later the neighbour's grandson gave Lucy's brother a small portable chest, saying that it belonged to the captain of the *St. John*. Whether this story is true or not, both the chest and letter are now on display at the Maritime Museum in Cohasset. The chest has a secret compartment and looks authentic. Other items from the *St. John* are on display in the Cohasset Museum, including Captain Oliver's writing desk, a limestone ballast and a masthead truck.[6]

Another story surrounding the *St. John* claims that there was a curse on the ship and its fate was sealed long before it set sail for America. The story goes that Colm Conneely, a brother of Tony Conneely from Lettermullen, the reported first captain of the ship, wanted to join the priesthood, but he either failed the entrance exam or was unable to raise the necessary college fees. So great was his disappointment that he renounced the Catholic faith and became an Anglican minister in England. He became acquainted with many influential people in England and it was through these connections that the finance to build the *St. John* is said to have been raised. At the time of the *St. John*'s fatal voyage, Tony Conneely was unable to sail as his wife was ill. Many conjectured that the sinking of the brig was God's way of punishing Colm Conneely for abandoning the Catholic religion. This story was recorded in an Irish book called *Stories of the Islands*, written by Peter Dirrane and published in 1929. However, another source states that Colm Conneely was not an Anglican minister and there are also those who believe that there was another ship named the *St. John* which may have been the 'cursed' ship; this was smaller vessel, supposedly built in Galway, but again this has never been proven.[7]

X

COMMEMORATION AND REMEMBRANCE

Henry David Thoreau's observations as he walked the Cohasset shoreline on 9 October 1849 are an important part of the *St. John* story. One wonders about Thoreau's own feelings about the sad event. He was not impressed with the funeral procession, confessing that if he had found a body 'cast up on the beach in some lonely place' it might have affected him more. IIis writings on the subject can either be interpreted as a show of indifference or as evidence of a strong belief in the will of God. The following words recorded by Thoreau commemorate, in a strange sort of way, the aftermath of the terrible disaster in October 1849:

I sympathized rather with the winds and waves, as if to toss and mangle these poor human bodies was the order of the day. If this was the law of Nature, why waste any time in awe or pity? If the last day were come, we should not think so much about the separation of friends or the blighted prospects of individuals. I saw that corpses might be multiplied, as on the field of battle, till they no longer affected us in any degree, as exceptions to the common lot of humanity. Take all the graveyards together, they are always the majority.

It is the individual and private that demands our sympathy. A man can attend but one funeral in the course of his life, can behold but one corpse. Yet I saw that the inhabitants of the shore would be not a little affected by this event. They would watch there many days and nights for the sea to give up its dead, and their imaginations and sympathies would supply the place of mourners far away, who as yet knew not of the wreck. Many days after this, something white was seen floating on the water by one who was sauntering on the beach. It was approached in a boat, and found to be the body of a woman, which had risen in an upright position, whose white cap was blown back with the wind. I saw that the beauty of the shore itself was wrecked for many a lonely walker there, until he could perceive, at last, how its beauty was enhanced by wrecks like this, and it acquired thus a rarer and sublimer beauty still.

Why care for these dead bodies? They really have no friends but the worms and fishes. Their owners were coming to the New World, as Columbus and the Pilgrims did, they were within a mile of its shores; but, before they could reach it, they emigrated to a newer world than ever Columbus dreamed of, yet one of whose existence we believe that there is far more universal and convincing evidence – though it has not yet been discovered by science – than Columbus had of this: not merely mariners' tales and some paltry drift-wood and seaweed, but a continual drift and instinct to all our shores. I saw their empty hulks that came to land; but they themselves, meanwhile, were cast upon some shore yet further west, toward which we are all tending, and which we shall reach at last, it may be through storm and darkness, as they did. No doubt, we have reason to thank God that they have not been 'shipwrecked into life again'.

The mariner who makes the safest port in Heaven, perchance, seems to his friends on earth to be shipwrecked, for they deem Boston Harbor the better place; though perhaps invisible to them, a skilful pilot comes to meet him, and the fairest and balmiest gales blow off that coast, his good ship makes the land in halcyon days, and he kisses the shore in rapture there, while his old hulk tosses in the surf here. It is hard to part with one's body, but, no doubt, it is easy to do without it when once it is gone. All their plans and hopes burst like a bubble! Infants by the score dashed on the rocks by the enraged Atlantic Ocean! No, no! If the St. John *did not make her port here, she had been telegraphed there. The strongest wind cannot stagger a Spirit; it is a Spirit's breath. A just man's purpose cannot be split on any Grampus or material rock, but itself will split rocks till it succeeds.*[1]

Most people need some sort of memorial to visit when remembering their departed loved ones. They take consolation in erecting headstones that record the deceased's name in stone and serve as a testimonial to their time in this world. But a monument or memorial was denied to those lost at sea or consigned to a mass

Wooden carving of the brig St. John *in the church in Lettermullen by Dermot Nestor. (Courtesy of Alice Scanlan)*

grave following the sinking of the *St. John*. Grief has far-reaching tentacles that can touch every corner of a nation, and a tragedy such as this affects not only the friends and family of those who are lost but also entire communities. The need to remember and commemorate tragic events becomes strong. While this need is not unique to Ireland, it is an important part of our way of life. This is perhaps a legacy of the famine. The mass exile of people during these troubled years exported our tragedy to other countries and bound other people to our plight. Links with Irish organisations already in existence in America were strengthened and their leaders lent their support to the immigrants.

The Ancient Order of Hibernians was adamant that a memorial be erected to commemorate the loss of the *St. John*. Eventually, on 26 May 1914 the Cohasset Central Cemetery authorities granted permission for a memorial to be erected close to the mass grave in memory of the victims. On 30 May 1914 the Ancient Order of Hibernians and the Ladies Auxiliary, the female branch of the order, had a twenty-foot Celtic cross erected near the site of the grave. It was placed at the top of a low hill that overlooked the ocean and the scene of the disaster. Thousands of people (some reports estimate between ten and twenty thousand) attended the dedication. The unveiling was conducted by Tessie St John, granddaughter of James St John, the man who married Mary Kane Cole, one of the survivors. The governor of Massachusetts, Hon. David I. Walsh, spoke at the ceremony and thanked the seven thousand Hibernians from all over Bay State for attending. Superintendent Philip Lothrop Towle of Cohasset General Cemetery later stated that the exact location of the mass grave was unknown because it had not been properly marked at the time of the

The St. John *celtic cross*
(Courtesy of John Costello)

tragedy. The cross was located just north of where the original burial ground was believed to be. It must be very close as it seems doubtful, given the enormity of the tragedy, that such a grave could be forgotten so quickly. The Ancient Order of Hibernians must have had evidence of the site in 1914. It is likely that confirmation regarding the location of the grave would have come from living memory. The inscription on the monument reads as follows:

> *This cross was erected and dedicated May 30, 1914 by the A.O.H. and the L.A.A.O.H. of Massachusetts to mark the final resting place of about forty-five Irish emigrants from a total company of ninety-nine who lost their lives on Grampus Ledge off Cohasset, October 7, 1849 in the wreck of the Brig* St. John *from Galway, Ireland. R.I.P.*[2]

On 21 August 1949, almost one hundred years after the brig *St. John* sank, Archbishop Cushing travelled to Cohasset to celebrate a solemn pontifical mass in memory of all who had lost their lives in the tragedy. It was celebrated on the grounds of St Anthony's church on South Main Street. Archbishop Cushing also sponsored a poetry competition for the anniversary of the disaster. Contestants were required to recount the tragic story of the *St. John* in verse. The winner was Professor Charles Brady of Canisius College, Buffalo; the runners-up included Herbert Kenny, Edward Myers and James Hanlon. A centenary commemoration booklet was produced for the anniversary mass. (Archbishop Cushing later became a cardinal and officially dedicated the Cathedral of Our Lady Assumed into Heaven and St Nicholas 'New Cathedral' in Galway city on 15 August 1965.) Below is a list of the priests who took part in the *St. John* centenary commemoration ceremony. Revd Michael J. Houlihan, listed below, was chaplain to the Ancient Order of Hibernians:

Revd Patrick J. Waters, Deacon of Honour to His Excellency

Revd Michael J. Houlihan, Deacon of Honour to His Excellency

Revd Michael J. Splain, Assisting Priest

Revd Thomas A. Flynn, Deacon of the Mass

Revd James F. Grimes, Sub-Deacon of the Mass

Revd Fredrick R. McManus, Master of Ceremonies

Revd Joseph Daley, Assistant Master of Ceremonies

Revd Joseph W. Leahy, Thurifer

Revd Francis S. Keany, Cross Bearer

Revd Francis D. Scully, Acolyte

Revd Ralph Enos, Acolyte

Revd Edward D. Tangney, Gremial Bearer

Revd Martin P. Harney, Bugia Bearer

Revd James F. Cassidy, Mitre Bearer

Revd John W. Mahoney, Crozier Bearer

Revd Patrick J. Flaherty, Book Bearer

Revd Edmund W. Croke, Torch Bearer

Revd John J. Kelly, Torch Bearer

Revd Thomas A. Dwyer, Torch Bearer

Revd Ambrose B. Flynn, Torch Bearer

Revd Frederick R. Condon, Choir Conductor

Revd William J. Desmond

Revd Lawrence Crowley

Mr Francis Regan, Train Bearer[3]

John Bhaba Jaick Ó Congaola of Lettermullen was the driving force behind a number of events that were arranged to commemorate the 150th anniversary of the tragedy.

His life-long interest in the disaster had begun as

a child, when he heard an old woman in Connemara telling the story of the brig *St. John*. He travelled to Boston in 1998 and requested that an anniversary committee be set up there, while he in turn would establish one in Ireland. The two committees, one in Boston and the other in Lettermullen, Connemara, were set up to raise awareness of the plight of the Irish during the famine and to organise a commemoration. The events were held on 9 and 10 October 1999. A reception was held in St Anthony's Parish Hall, Cohasset, and included a short historical presentation on the *St. John*. A commemorative journal was also produced containing advertisements from businesses that supported the events. Support came from both sides of the Atlantic and the proceeds were donated to charity. During a social evening of music and song, held in the Teacher's Union Hall, Dorchester, John Bhaba Jaick Ó Congaola presented the Boston Brig *St. John* committee with a model of a *pucán*, a traditional Irish sailing vessel. At 3 p.m. on 10 October the anniversary mass was celebrated by Fr Bernard Law (today a cardinal) in Saint Anthony's church, Cohasset. Following the mass, a boat trip to Grampus Ledge and Minot's Lighthouse was organised. A wreath-laying ceremony also took place in Cohasset cemetery.

A documentary film about the *St. John* and the events surrounding its tragic end was broadcast on the *Seán Folan Show* in Boston and recordings of it were later made available to the public. It is also hoped that a famine memorial will be opened near Mutton Island Lighthouse in Galway and dedicated to the memory of all those who fled starvation and disease during the Irish famine.[4]

The following poem to the memory of the famine victims was discovered among the John Bhaba Jaick Ó Congaola collection, but no author was recorded for this very poignant work.

'To Their Memory'

How many died in forty-five,
The first year of the hunger?
When starvation cursed the old ones first,
And then tormented the younger.

And when we cried as the praties died,
And turned black in the soil;

Who was there to hear our prayer
For food that was not spoiled?

And where was God when the Irish sod
Gave up its putrid yield,
And the sickening smell of a crop from hell
Came up from every field.

'Twas not God's hand that cursed the land,
But the hand of a human master,
Who turned his back when the spuds turned black,
And created that awful disaster.

For the landlord's fields gave abundant yields,
But we Irish could not afford it;
So fathers and sons were held off with guns
While the harvested crop was exported.

And the men of renown, who worked for the crown,
To administer public care,
Heard our plea from across the sea,
And pretended that we weren't there.

How many fell sick in forty-six
When the potato failed again,

And malnutrition on frail conditions
Claimed children, women and men.

And what intent had the government?
Did they try to ease our pain?
Or did they try to keep prices high
By forbidding the import of grain.

The only food that they didn't exclude
Was American Indian maize;
For it posed no rival to the landlord's survival,
And for that it was given high praise.

But America warned that Indian corn
Was too hard, and had to be grated;
But they gave it away to the poor anyway,
And it cut through our bellies like razors.

Then, when a man died, his children and bride
Were sent to the workhouse for hire,
Where lice and fleas spread dreadful disease,
And fever set them on fire.

Again we implored, and again they ignored
As our dead were hauled off in carts.

Uncaring, they slept, while mothers wept;
And their apathy hardened our hearts.

Then, dear God in heaven, came black forty-seven,
A year that in horror still stands;
For the crown ordained that the landlords maintain
The tenants who lived on their lands.

So what did they do, these faithful and true,
Defenders of church and of crown;
They dispossessed our families like pests,
And tore our wee cottages down.

With no fixed abodes, we wandered the roads
Through the fiercest winter in years;
Clad only in rags; our possessions in bags;
With nothing to taste but our tears.

Wracked with pain we wandered the lanes
In search of berries and roots;
'Til the crown rushed through an evening curfew,
And arrested all those on the loose.

Alone and forsaken, our women were taken,
And sent as indentured servants,

To lands far away from their own native clay,
In spite of their pleas, grim and fervent.

And pity the children, the innocent children,
Whose parents were laid in their graves;
Too young to pay rent, they were hastily sent
To factories and sweatshops like slaves.

Then came the date in forty-eight
When the landlords, cruel and clever,
To avoid being forced to absorb further cost
Discarded their tenants forever.

They consigned us to trips aboard coffin ships,
Not suited for man nor for beast;
In holds dark and damp, we were crowded and
    cramped:
The living beside the deceased.

And as we lay dying; some praying, some crying,
Like lifeless cargo, all stacked,
The ship's rolling motion across the wide ocean,
Made our empty bellies contract.

*Thousands were drowned on the ships that went
    down,
Never again to be seen;
If tombstones were floated for each death noted,
You could walk from Brooklyn to Skibbereen.*

*We barely survived on the ships that arrived
In the new land across the wide seas;
But weary and sore, we were stopped at the door,
For they said that we carried disease.*

*As the Banshee keened, we were quarantined,
And more came on every wave;
Then, some were freed; alone and in need,
While the rest found American graves.*

*Then came the time in forty-nine
When the rest of the world grew critical,
And loudly decried such genocide
For reasons that were only political.*

*So the government tried to stem the tide
Of the world's admonishing blast,
By producing a few potatoes that grew,
And declaring the crisis had passed.*

But the official's voice didn't make us rejoice
That the land had finally been blessed;
For as we chewed on nettles, our spuds fed their
*   cattle,*
For by now, we'd been all dispossessed.

Then came the group with the watered down soup
To set up their charity kitchen;
But the price was too high, for to qualify
We would have to give up our religion.

To see parents denying, as children were dying,
To take the soup or the porridge,
Was both demonstration and documentation
Of a people's faith, and their courage.

No matter who stated the crisis abated,
We still knew disease and starvation,
'Til the final aid that helped it to fade
Came from Irish in far away nations.

They'd dispersed our kin to the stormy winds,
And that became our salvation;
For though they tried to commit genocide,
They failed to achieve liquidation.

And to our defence came our own emigrants,
Now scattered all over the earth;
Who'd improved their lot, but never forgot
The land that had given them birth.

Sisters and brothers wrote back to their mothers,
Or any one they had left living;
Each letter returning as much of their earnings
As they could afford to be giving.

And the greedy and sinister government ministers,
Who'd thought that they'd finally erased us,
Were astonished to learn that our sons would return,
And that in the end was what braced us.

Today we recall the memory of all
The disease, the starvation and sorrow;
Of those who perished for the faith they cherished
And the hope of a better tomorrow.

But let not our fate, be guided by hate,
For the lord will have taken fair vengeance;
Remember instead, our own Irish dead,
And say a prayer in silent remembrance.[5]

LIST OF THE BRIG ST. JOHN'S PASSENGERS AND CREW

While most sources estimate the number of victims of the *St. John* tragedy to be ninety-nine and the survivors twenty-two, there are others who place the death toll as high as one hundred and forty-six. In fact, Northern Maritime Research Canada places the loss of life somewhere between one hundred and forty-four and one hundred and sixty-four people. Various sources also report a different figure for that of the survivors. One of these reports, which was published in the *Galway Vindicator*, suggests that there were between twenty and thirty more passengers on board the *St. John* than was declared in the manifest. *The Boston Post* reported that two of the survivors accused Captain Oliver of falsifying the list of passengers, claiming that there were an additional twenty or thirty people listed in a memorandum book that the captain kept in his personal possession. Another puzzling aspect of the disaster is the disappearance of the ship's official manifest. Was it lost during the storm? Was it deliberately left behind so that the actual number of passengers on board would remain unknown? It may never be known, but what is certain is that there were more people on board the *St. John* that terrible night than was recorded in the official documents.[1]

The main list of passengers available today seems to have been compiled by an American reporter. It contains more details regarding the victims from Clare than those from Galway. This would indicate that whoever supplied the information was more familiar with the Clare contingent on board. It is evident from the list that follows that the reporter who recorded the names had some difficulty understanding the Irish accent, resulting in errors in the spelling of names and addresses. Additional errors are also believed to have occurred when the list was sent to the printers, where the reporter's 'longhand' writing was misread. The following are examples of such errors. The first two letters of the name Flannigan were misread as the letter H. One woman, a Margaret Keenan, seems to have been recorded twice under two spelling variations of Ennistymon. Confusion surrounds the first name of Honora or Mary Burke; some sources also spell her name as Honour. For this listing she is recorded as Honora (Mary) Burke. Peggy Mullen was recorded as Meggy Mullen; this has also been corrected. Most sources record one of the surviving sailors as William Larkin; however, *The Boston Mail* recorded him as John. Other differences arise in the same newspaper. James Moran is recorded as James Morgan. Winny Galvin is recorded as Minny Galvin. Miss Brooks is recorded as Mrs Brooks. Andrew Frost is recorded as Andrew Forrest. One of the surviving sailors, Henry O'Hern is not recorded in the newspaper at all. The three Mulkenan sisters are recorded as Mulkennan. In the cabin passenger list there is a Margaret Flannigan – could this be Mary Flannigan? In the same section an N. Flannigan is listed – could this be Nancy Hannagan? Martha Perky's name appeared as Martha Purky and it was stated that she was related to Peggy Purky. There are three persons named McDarratt recorded, but these are possibly McDermott.[2]

Spelling errors also occurred in place names with different variations of the same name being recorded. These variations are included in the list along with the names believed to be correct, such as Ennistymon/

Inistivan/Innistivan, and so on. There are obviously other misspellings recorded on the list of the victims, but as there were no records available to identify the correct spellings, they will remain as they were first recorded.[3]

The following are examples of survivors who were not listed among the passengers or crew: Mrs Quinlan, recorded in the writings of Elizabeth Lothrop; the infant saved by Captain Lothrop; Martin and Patrick Flaherty (brothers); and a second Patrick Flaherty, all of whom returned to Lettermullen. If the brig *St. John* did indeed anchor off the coast of Lettermullen to take on water and extra passengers shortly after first setting sail, then the names of these additional passengers were not recorded. This being the case, there were more people on board than were listed in the ship's manifest. *The Boston Mail* records a Benjamin O'Brien as a surviving sailor, but he is not recorded in any other sources. M. Rootching is also recorded among the passengers saved, but he too is not recorded in any other source.[4]

On the day after the disaster, Newcomb Bates (Jr), the town clerk of Cohasset, recorded some additional names that do not appear on any other list. They included Catherine Fitzgerald, Bridget Muligan, Mary Freeman and Sally Sweeney, whose body was found 'calm and placid'. Nine of Patrick and Mary Sweeney's eleven children were named in *The Boston Mail*, November 1849 and later by a local source in Lettermullen, who was also in a position to name a tenth. Was Sally Sweeney a member of this family? There were two people named Miles Sweeney on board, one of whom was a child, and the son of Patrick and Mary Sweeney. Peggy Adams is recorded in the *Boston Daily Herald*; her sister arrived in Cohasset just as the funeral was about to take place. The following are additional names reported by *The Boston Mail*: Mary Joyce and her child, Mary Curtain, Peter Greally, Jas Greally, Pat Corcoran, Catherine McMahon, Thomas Donnelly, Bridget Doherty, Nappy Fahy, B. Kennelly or Conlin and three children. Nappy is a shortened version of the name Penelope. All of the additional names have been included in the list that follows, under the title 'Place of origin unknown'.[5]

Crew Survivors

Comerford, First Mate Henry (Galway)

Comerford, Isaac (Galway)

Flaherty, James (Lettermullen, Connemara, County Galway)

Frost, Andrew (Galway)

Kennelly, Michael (Galway)

Larkin, William (Galway)

O'Brien, Benjamin (Galway)

O'Hern, Henry (Galway)

Oliver, Captain Martin (Galway)

Walker, Thomas (Galway)

Crew Lost

Angiers, William

Connors, Michael

Kennelly, Edward

McDonough, Antonio

Thompson, William

– Two unnamed apprentice boys

Passenger Survivors

Burke, Honora (Mary) (aged 27)

Cole, Mary Kane (aged 24)

Cullen, Honora (aged 28)

Fitzpatrick, Michael (aged 26)

Flaherty, Martin (Lettermullen, Connemara, County Galway)

Flaherty, Patrick (Lettermullen, Connemara, County Galway)

Flaherty, Patrick (Lettermullen, Connemara, County Galway)

Flanagan, Catherine (aged 20)

Gibbon, Michael (aged 26)

Higgins, Betsy (aged 21)

Kearn, Austin (aged 20)

Kennelly, Barbara (aged 20)

Quinlan, Mrs (Place of origin unknown/lost)

Redding, Michael (aged 24)

Rootching, M. (Place of origin unknown/lost)

Slattery, Mary (aged 20)

– The infant saved by Captain Lothrop (Place of origin unknown/lost)

Passengers Lost

Adams, Peggy, steerage passenger (Place of origin unknown/lost)

Belton, John, steerage passenger (Galway)

*Brooks, Ms, steerage passenger (Ennistymon/
Inistivan/Innistivan, County Clare)*

*Burnes, Catherine, steerage passenger (Lahinch/
Inch/Anch, County Clare)*

Burke, Bridget, steerage passenger (Galway)

Burke, Thomas, steerage passenger (Galway)

Butler, John, steerage passenger (Galway)

*Byrnes, Daniel, steerage passenger (Lahinch/Inch/
Anch, County Clare)*

Cahill, Mary, steerage passenger (Galway)

*Connelly, Bridget, steerage passenger (Connemara/
Kunnamara, County Galway)*

*Corcoran, Pat, steerage passenger (Place of origin
unknown/lost)*

Corman, Patrick, steerage passenger (Galway)

*Curtain, Mary, steerage passenger (Place of origin
unknown/lost)*

Curtis, Mary, steerage passenger (County Clare)

*Doherty, Bridget, steerage passenger (Place of
origin unknown/lost)*

Dolan, John, steerage passenger (Galway)

Dolan, Mary, steerage passenger (Galway)

Donnelly, Honora, steerage passenger (Galway)

Donnelly, Thomas, steerage passenger (Place of origin unknown/lost)

Egan, Bridget, steerage passenger (Ennis, Innes, County Clare)

Egan, Honor, steerage passenger (Ennis, Innes, County Clare)

Egan, Michael, steerage passenger (Ennis, Innes, County Clare)

Fahy, Nappy, steerage passenger (Place of origin unknown/lost)

Fahey, Bridget, steerage passenger (Galway)

Fahey, Martha, steerage passenger (Galway)

Fahey, Thomas, steerage passenger (Galway)

Fitzgerald, Catherine, steerage passenger (Place of origin unknown/lost)

Fitzpatrick, Catherine, steerage passenger (Galway)

Flannigan, Mary, cabin passenger (Kilfenora/ Kilnare/Kilnara, County Clare)

Freeman, Mary (and child), steerage passenger (Ennis, Innes, County Clare)

Frowley, Mary (and child), steerage passengers (Roan, County Clare)

Galvin, Mary, steerage passenger (Kilmurry/ Kilmary, County Clare)

Galvin, Winny, steerage passenger (Kilmurry/
Kilmary, County Clare)

Glynn, Hugh, steerage passenger (Ennistymon/
Inistivan/Innistivan, County Clare)

Greally, Jas., steerage passenger (Place of origin
unknown/lost)

Greally, Peter, steerage passenger (Place of origin
unknown/lost)

Griffin, Michael, steerage passenger (Lahinch/
Inch/Anch, County Clare)

Hannagan, Margaret, cabin passenger (Kilfenora/
Kilnare/Kilnara, County Clare)

Hannagan, Michael, steerage passenger (Lalinen,
County Clare)

Hannagan, Nancy, cabin passenger (Kilfenora/
Kilnare/Kilnara, County Clare)

Hassett, Ellen, steerage passenger (Lahinch/Inch/
Anch, County Clare)

Henniff, Catherine (and sister), steerage passenger
(Galway)

Joyce, Mary (and child), steerage passengers (Place
of origin unknown/lost)

Kane, Margaret (and child), steerage passenger
(Kilmurry/Kilmary, County Clare)

*Keenan, Margaret, steerage passenger (Ennistymon/
Inistivan/Innistivan, County Clare)*

*Kennelly (or Conlin) B. (and three children), steerage
passengers (Place of origin unknown/lost)*

*Lahiff (or Rohan), Honora, steerage passenger
(County Clare)*

*Lahiff (or Rohan), John, steerage passenger
(County Clare)*

*Lahiff, John, steerage passenger (Kilfenora/
Kilnare/Kilanara, County Clare)*

*Lahiff, Patrick, steerage passenger (Kilfenora/
Kilnare/Kilanara, County Clare)*

Landsky, Mary, steerage passenger (Galway)

*McDermott, Joyce (and child), steerage passengers
(Galway)*

McDermott, Mary, steerage passenger (Galway)

*McGrath, James, steerage passenger (Kilmurry/
Kilmary, County Clare)*

*McGrath, Patrick, steerage passenger (Kilmurry/
Kilmary, County Clare)*

*McMahon, Bridget, steerage passenger (Roan,
County Clare)*

*McMahon, Catherine, steerage passenger (Place of
origin unknown/lost)*

McMahon, Patrick, *steerage passenger (Roan, County Clare)*

McNamara, Mary, *steerage passenger (Kilmurry/ Kilmary, County Clare)*

Madigan, Hugh, *steerage passenger (Ennistymon/ Inistivan/Innistivan, County Clare)*

Maddigan, Bridget, *steerage passenger (Kilfenora/ Kilnare/Kilanara, County Clare)*

Malloy, Peggy, *steerage passenger (Lahinch/Inch/ Anch, County Clare)*

Moran, James, *steerage passenger (Dysart/Dyant, County Clare)*

Mulkenan, Honora, *steerage passenger (County Clare)*

Mulkenan, Margaret, *steerage passenger (County Clare)*

Mulkenan, Mary, *steerage passenger (County Clare)*

Mullen, Honora, *steerage passenger (Galway)*

Mullen, Peggy (and her sister's child), *steerage passengers (Galway)*

Muligan, Bridget, *steerage passenger (Place of origin unknown/lost)*

Murphy, Jeremiah, *steerage passenger (Dysart/ Dyant, County Clare)*

Nolan, Mary, steerage passenger (Roan, County Clare)

Noonan, Patrick, steerage passenger (Galway)

O'Brien, Eliza, cabin passenger (Ennistymon/ Inistivan/Innistivan, County Clare)

Purky, Martha, steerage passenger (Galway)

Purky, Peggy, steerage passenger (Galway)

Quinn, Bridget, cabin passenger (Ennistymon/ Inistivan/Innistivan, County Clare)

Riley, Thomas, steerage passenger (Kilfenora/ Kilnare/Kilanara, County Clare)

Sexton, Martin, steerage passenger (Dysart/ Dyant, County Clare)

Slattery, Ann, steerage passenger (Ennistymon/ Inistivan/Innistivan, County Clare)

Slattery, Bridget, steerage passenger (Ennistymon/ Inistivan/Innistivan, County Clare)

Sweeney, Agnes, steerage passenger (Lettercallow, Connemara, County Galway)

Sweeney, Bridget, steerage passenger (Lettercallow, Connemara, County Galway)

Sweeney, Catherine, steerage passenger (Lettercallow, Connemara, County Galway)

Sweeney, John, steerage passenger (Lettercallow,

Connemara, County Galway)

Sweeney, Joseph, steerage passenger (Lettercallow,
Connemara, County Galway)

Sweeney, Mary, steerage passenger (Lettercallow,
Connemara, County Galway)

Sweeney, Mary (daughter), steerage passenger
(Lettercallow, Connemara, County Galway)

Sweeney, Miles, steerage passenger (Lettercallow,
Connemara, County Galway)

Sweeney, Miles, steerage passenger (Galway)

Sweeney, Patrick, steerage passenger (Lettercallow,
Connemara, County Galway)

Sweeney, Patrick Jr, steerage passenger
(Lettercallow, Connemara, County Galway)

Sweeney, Sally, steerage passenger (Place of origin
unknown/lost)

Sweeney, Sarah, steerage passenger (Lettercallow,
Connemara, County Galway)

Sweeney, Thomas, steerage passenger
(Lettercallow, Connemara, County Galway)

– Honora (Mary) Burke's three children, steerage
passengers (Place of origin unknown/lost)

– Honora Cullen's three children, steerage
passengers (Place of origin unknown/lost)[6]

Crew saved: 10 – Passengers saved: 17
Crew lost: 7 – Passengers lost: 109
Total on board: 143

EPILOGUE

In 1803 the British government introduced legislation to protect emigrant passengers, and during the decades that followed this legislation matured and evolved. However, the laws were not always enforceable and unscrupulous shipowners and shipmasters continually found ways of evading them. These infringements paved the way for corrupt maritime businessmen to exploit their passengers and capitalise on their misery. Nevertheless, in the years following the famine conditions improved and passengers experienced a much more comfortable voyage in comparison to the unfortunate people who had fled Ireland in the 1840s. Regulations were put in place to determine the maximum number of passengers that a ship could carry, and to ensure that sufficient food and water was provided for the voyage. However, it was too late for almost one million Irish men, women and children who had fled the country during the famine.

Between 1845 and 1850, some 100,000 Irish people

arrived in Boston. They took any work they could find and lived in squalid tenements while struggling to keep their families alive. Life proved very difficult for the Irish in the early years and wasn't rendered any easier by the bigotry of the locals. Signs declaring 'No Irish Need Apply' became ubiquitous in the windows of businesses and boarding houses, and the immigrants struggled to secure employment. But in spite of this many of them later succeeded in reaching the highest offices and positions in their adopted country. It was the descendants of this scorned refugee population who helped create a new, powerful force in America.[1] Nothing deterred this impoverished yet spirited generation who succeeded in transforming themselves from destitute foreigners into successful business people. That they managed to overcome the numerous obstacles placed before them is a testament of their strength and endurance. Many of them became leaders in the fields of politics, arts, sports, religion and business.

In 1849, Patrick Kennedy, progenitor of the Kennedy dynasty, sailed from Wexford to the United States on board *The Washington Irving*; it was the same year as the brig *St. John* sailed from Galway. His grandson, John F. Kennedy, went on to become one of the most famous presidents of the United States. John F. Kennedy never forgot his Irish roots and he once said, 'We are a nation of immigrants … the experience of our ancestors paves the way for our achievements.' Another famous Irish-American was Henry Ford, founder of the automobile industry. His father left Cork for Quebec in 1847, and eventually made his way to Detroit.[2]

Today, some forty million Americans claim to have Irish ancestry. A large percentage of these people maintain that their ancestors arrived in the United States during the famine. In Boston alone over twenty per cent of the population are Irish-American, giving rise to a flourishing community, with countless Gaelic football teams, Irish gift stores, pubs and radio and television programmes. On Sunday, 28 June 1998, The Irish Famine Memorial Park, at the corner of School and Washington Streets, was dedicated, forever 'enshrining a timeless tale of tragedy and triumph'.

It has been a long and arduous journey through time and space since Henry David Thoreau wrote these final words on the Cohasset shoreline:

This rocky shore is called Pleasant Cove on some maps; on the map of Cohasset, the name appears to be confined to the particular cove where I saw the wreck of the St. John. *The ocean did not look, now, as if any were ever shipwrecked in it; it was not grand and sublime, but beautiful as a lake. Not a vestige of a wreck was visible, nor could I believe that the bones of many a shipwrecked man were buried in that pure sand.*[3]

APPENDIX

List of Famine Ships that advertised in and serviced Galway 1845–1850

Abbotsford

Albion

Alice

Amphetrite

Argimou

Barbara

Bethel

Cambyses

Caractacus

Caroline

Carolina

Cashmere

Celeste

C. H. Appelton

Charlotte

Clarence

Clytha

Coldstream

Commence

Corrib

Cremona

Cushlamachree

Daniel

David

Delphin

Doctor Kneises

Downes

Eliza Ann

Elizabeth Hughes

Emma Prescott

Emmeline

Fanny

Francis–Watts

GEM

G. W. Brinkerhoff

G. W. Laurence

Haidee

Helen

Helena

Henderson

H. Mellon

IHN John

Irvine

Islam

John Begg

John Clifford

Josephine

Joshua Carroll

Kate

Laing

Lelia

Linden

Lively

Lord Fitzgerald

Lord Fitzroy

Lyna

Malvina

Manchester

Margaret Milne

Maria

Marine Plant

Martha

Messenger

M. Howes

Minerva

Nancy

Napoleon

Northumberland

Ohio

Orwell Lass

Pacific

Pageant

Plant

Preciosa

Rebecca

Redwing

Regina

Robert Alexander Parke

Russia E. D.

Sarah Milledge

Seabird	Thomas Baker
St. George	Valhalla
St. John	Viceroy
Tassie	Victoria
Thalia	Wakefield
The Arab	Walkella
The Asia	W. H. Spear
The Lucullus	William Kerry
The Medora	XL
Thetis	Young Queen

NOTES

Chapter I

1. Henry, William, *Role of Honour: The Mayors of Galway City 1485–2001* (2001), pp. 102, 103.
   Litton, Helen, *The Irish Famine: An Illustrated History* (1994), Introduction.
   Ó Cathaoir, Brendan, *Famine Diary* (1999), Introduction.
   O'Dowd, Peadar, *The Great Famine and the West 1845–1850* (1995), pp. 2, 3.
   The Illustrated London News: 'The Galway Starvation Riots' (25-6-1842).

2. Henry, William, *Role of Honour: The Mayors of Galway City 1485–2001* (2001), p. 93.
   Litton, Helen, *The Irish Famine: An Illustrated History* (1994), pp. 9, 10, 12, 13, 15.
   O'Dowd, Peadar, *The Great Famine and the West 1845–1850* (1995), p. 3.
   The Galway Mercury: 'The Devon Commission' (26-6-1847).

3. *Boston Herald*: 'Triumph out of Tragedy – Commemorating the 150 Anniversary of the Great Hunger' (26-6-1998), p. 3.

Litton, Helen, *The Irish Famine: An Illustrated History* (1994), p. 17.

Ó Cathaoir, Brendan, *Famine Diary* (1999), pp. 3, 4.

O'Dowd, Peadar, *The Great Famine and the West 1845–1850* (1995), p. 3.

The Dublin Evening Post (9-9-1845).

4. *Boston Herald*, 'Triumph out of Tragedy – Commemorating the 150 Anniversary of the Great Hunger' (26-6-1998), p. 3.
    Litton, Helen, *The Irish Famine: An Illustrated History* (1994), pp. 30, 43.
    Ó Cathaoir, Brendan, *Famine Diary* (1999), p. 5.
    Woodham-Smith, Cecil, *The Great Hunger 1845–1849* (1989), p. 58.

5. *The Galway Mercury*: 'Irish Sufferings – Whig and Tory Sympathy' (5-6-1847).

Chapter II

1. *The Illustrated London News*: 'Famine and Starvation in the County of Cork' (16-1-1847); 'Mortality in Skibbereen' (30-1-1846); Mr James Mahony, 'Sketches in the West of Ireland' (13/20-2-1847); 'The Late Food Riots in Ireland' (7-11-1846); 'The Potato Disease' (18-10-1845).

2. *The Illustrated London News*: 'Famine and Starvation in the County of Cork' (16-1-1847); 'Mortality in Skibbereen' (30-1-1846); Mr James Mahony, 'Sketches in the West of Ireland' (13/20-2-1847).

3. *The Illustrated London News*: 'Famine and Starvation in the County of Cork' (16-1-1847); 'Mortality in Skibbereen' (30-1-1846); Mr James Mahony, 'Sketches in the West of Ireland' (13/20-2-1847).

4. *The Illustrated London News*: 'Famine and Starvation in the County of Cork' (16-1-1847); 'Mortality in Skibbereen' (30-1-1846); Mr James Mahony, 'Sketches in the West of Ireland' (13/20-2-1847).

5. Litton, Helen, *The Irish Famine: An Illustrated History* (1994), pp. 104, 105, 108.

6. *The Galway Mercury*: 'A Famine Report' (13-3-1847). *The Illustrated London News*: A Poem (13-2-1847).

Chapter III

1. *Boston Irish Reporter*: 'Cohasset Monument Honors Famine Victims' (October 1996). *Boston Sunday Herald*: 'Cohasset Ceremony Recalls Shipwreck' (10-10-1999).

2. *Boston Irish Reporter*: 'Cohasset Monument Honors Famine Victims' (October 1996). *Boston Sunday Herald*: 'Cohasset Ceremony Recalls Shipwreck' (10-10-1999). Kennedy, M., 'The Winter Voyages of the Famine Ships *Cushlamachree* and *Londonderry*'. *Illustrated London News* (8-5-1847).

3. *Boston Irish Reporter*: 'Cohasset Monument Honors Famine Victims' (October 1996).
    Boston Sunday Herald: 'Cohasset Ceremony Recalls Shipwreck' (10-10-1999).
    Litton, Helen, *The Irish Famine: An Illustrated History* (1994), pp. 105, 107.
    Ó Cathaoir, Brendan, *Famine Diary* (1999), pp. 123, 131, 149.

4. Cunningham, John, '*A Town Tormented by the Sea*': Galway *1790-1914* (2004), pp. 155, 156.
    Internet Articles: http://www.islayinfo.com/Exmouth-islay-tragedy.html, 'Emigrant Ship Exmouth.'
    Kennedy, M., 'The Winter Voyages of the Famine Ships *Cushlamachree* and *Londonderry*.'
    Litton, Helen, *The Irish Famine: An Illustrated History* (1994), pp. 105, 107.
    Ó Cathaoir, Brendan, *Famine Diary* (1999), pp. 123, 131, 149.

5. Cunningham, John, '*A Town Tormented by the Sea*': Galway *1790-1914* (2004), pp. 155, 156.
    Internet Articles: http://www.islayinfo.com/Exmouth-islay-tragedy.html, 'Emigrant Ship Exmouth'.
    Kennedy, M., 'The Winter Voyages of the Famine Ships *Cushlamachree* and *Londonderry*'.
    Litton, Helen, *The Irish Famine: An Illustrated History* (1994), pp. 105, 107.
    Ó Cathaoir, Brendan, *Famine Diary* (1999), pp. 123, 131, 149.

6. *Boston Irish Reporter*: 'Cohasset Monument Honors Famine Victims' (October 1996).
Boston Sunday Herald: 'Cohasset Ceremony Recalls Shipwreck' (10-10-1999).
Cunningham, John, '*A Town Tormented by the Sea*': Galway *1790-1914* (2004), pp. 155, 156.
The Galway Mercury: 'Irish Sufferings – Whig and Tory Sympathy' (5-6-1847).

Chapter IV

1. *Boston Herald*: 'Triumph out of Tragedy – Commemorating the 150 Anniversary of the Great Hunger' (26-6-1998), p. 3.

2. *Boston Herald*: 'Triumph out of Tragedy – Commemorating the 150 Anniversary of the Great Hunger' (26-6-1998), p. 3.
Garvey, Fr G., *Bushypark Celebrates 1837-1987* (1988), p. 8.
The Galway Mercury: 'Starvation – Inquest' (13-3-1847); 'More Deaths by Starvation' (22-1-1848).

3. Garvey, Fr G., *Bushypark Celebrates 1837-1987* (1988), p. 8.
The Galway Mercury: 'Starvation – Inquest' (13-3-1847); 'More Deaths by Starvation' (22-1-1848).

4. Cunningham, John, '*A Town Tormented by the Sea*': Galway *1790-1914* (2004), p. 154.
Galway Advertiser: 'The Workhouse' (3-3-1994).
Garvey, Fr G., *Bushypark Celebrates 1837-1987* (1988), p. 8.

The Connacht Tribune: 'The Great Famine, Tribune Extra' (24-3-1995).

The Galway Mercury: 'Starvation – Inquest' (13-3-1847).

5. O'Dowd, Peadar, *The Great Famine and the West 1845-1850* (1995), p. 19.

    Ó hÉideáin, Eustás, *The Dominicans in Galway 1241-1991* (1991), p. 96.

6. *Boston Herald*: 'Triumph out of Tragedy – Commemorating the 150 Anniversary of the Great Hunger' (26-6-1998), p. 3.

    Cunningham, John, '*A Town Tormented by the Sea': Galway 1790-1914* (2004), p. 157.

    Galway Advertiser: 'When Galway Starved' (27-6-1996).

    Lecture: 'The Brig *St. John* Disaster 1849' by John Bhaba Jaick Ó Congaola, Ennis, County Clare (29-1-2007).

    Murray, James P., *Galway: A Medico-Social History* (1994), pp. 50, 51.

    The Galway Mercury: 'The Song of the Famine' (10-7-1847).

Chapter V

1. Cunningham, John, '*A Town Tormented by the Sea': Galway 1790-1914* (2004), p. 157.

    O'Cathaoir, Brendan, *Famine Diary* (1999), pp. 137, 138.

    O'Dowd, Peadar, *Galway City* (1998), p. 49.

    The Galway Mercury: 'Emigration' (1-5-1847); 'Passage Across the Atlantic' (19-6-1847).

2. *Brig* St. John *of Galway was Cohasset's Worst Shipwreck,*
   Cohasset Historical Society. John Bhaba Jaick Ó
   Congaola collection.
   Comber, H., *The Book of Thomas J. Comber and Eliza
   Comerford* (n.d.), p. 2. John Bhaba Jaick Ó Congaola
   collection.
   Cunningham, John, '*A Town Tormented by the Sea': Galway
   1790-1914* (2004), p. 155.
   Lloyd's Register and Supplement: 1845, 1846, 1847, 1850.
   Notes copied from Newcomb Bates (Jr), the Town Clerk
   of (Cohasset) (7-10-1849).
   David Wadsworth (The curator of the Cohasset Historical
   Society), 'Information Relating to the "*St. John*" wreck' (8-
   3-1984). John Bhaba Jaick Ó Congaola collection.

3. *The Boston Post*: 'Brig *St. John* of Galway – List of
   Survivors and Drowned' (12-10-1849).
   Brig St. John of Galway was Cohasset's Worst Shipwreck,
   Cohasset Historical Society. John Bhaba Jaick Ó
   Congaola collection.
   Notes copied from Newcomb Bates (Jr), the Town Clerk
   of (Cohasset) (7-10-1849).
   The Boston Mail: 'Wreck of the *St. John*' (3-11-1849).
   The Galway Mercury: 'Wreck of the *St. John*' (11-10-1849).

4. *Boston Irish Reporter*: 'Cohasset Monument Honors
   Famine Victims' (October 1996).
   Brig St. John *of Galway was Cohasset's Worst Shipwreck,*
   Cohasset Historical Society. John Bhaba Jaick Ó
   Congaola collection.

Interview: John Bhaba Jaick Ó Congaola (18-7-2008).

5. *Boston Irish Reporter*: 'Cohasset Monument Honors
    Famine Victims' (October 1996).
    Brig St. John *of Galway was Cohasset's Worst Shipwreck*,
    Cohasset Historical Society. John Bhaba Jaick Ó
    Congaola collection.
    The Boston Daily Herald: 'The Burial of the Victims of the
    St. John – Melancholy Sight' (12-10-1849).
    The Galway Mercury: 'Song of the Famine' (5-9-1846).
    The Patriot Ledger: 'Ceremonies to Honor Irish Shipwreck
    Victims' (6-10-1999).

Chapter VI

1. *Boston Irish Reporter*: 'Cohasset Monument Honors
    Famine Victims' (October 1996).
    Brig St. John *of Galway was Cohasset's Worst Shipwreck*,
    Cohasset Historical Society. John Bhaba Jaick Ó
    Congaola collection.
    Ennistymon Parish Magazine, 'The Shipwreck of the *St.
    John*'. Article compiled from material supplied by Brud
    Slattery, John Flanagan (both Lahinch), and Frank
    Flanagan (USA) (1996).
    The Galway Mercury: 'Awful Shipwreck at Minot's Ledge
    – Loss of *St. John* of Galway – About One Hundred
    Drowned – Men, Women and Children' (27-10-1849).

2. *Boston Irish Reporter*: 'Cohasset Monument Honors
    Famine Victims' (October 1996).

Fraser, Robert, *Cohasset Vignettes* (1981).
Ennistymon Parish Magazine, 'The Shipwreck of the *St. John*'. Article compiled from material supplied by Brud Slattery, John Flanagan (both Lahinch), and Frank Flanagan (USA) (1996).

3. *Boston Irish Reporter*: 'Cohasset Monument Honors Famine Victims' (October 1996).
   Brig St. John *of Galway was Cohasset's Worst Shipwreck*, Cohasset Historical Society. John Bhaba Jaick Ó Congaola collection.
   Ennistymon Parish Magazine, 'The Shipwreck of the *St. John*'. Article compiled from material supplied by Brud Slattery, John Flanagan (both Lahinch), and Frank Flanagan (USA) (1996).
   Miscellaneous articles and letters from the John Bhaba Jaick Ó Congaola collection: 'The Wreck of the Brig *St. John*'.

4. *Boston Irish Reporter*: 'Cohasset Monument Honors Famine Victims' (October 1996).
   Brig St. John *of Galway was Cohasset's Worst Shipwreck*, Cohasset Historical Society. John Bhaba Jaick Ó Congaola collection.
   Ennistymon Parish Magazine, 'The Shipwreck of the *St. John*'. Article compiled from material supplied by Brud Slattery, John Flanagan (both Lahinch), and Frank Flanagan (USA) (1996).
   The Boston Irish Echo: Paddy Mulkerrins, 'More on the Ill-fated Brig, *St. John* – Remembers the *St. John*' (14-4-

1984); Bill Loughran, 'More on the Ill-fated Brig, *St. John*' (14-4-1984).

The Galway Vindicator: 'Awful Shipwreck at Minot's Ledge – Loss of *St. John* of Galway – About One Hundred Drowned – Men, Women and Children' (3-11-1849).

5. *Boston Irish Reporter*: 'Cohasset Monument Honors Famine Victims' (October 1996).

Ennistymon Parish Magazine, 'The Shipwreck of the *St. John*'. Article compiled from material supplied by Brud Slattery, John Flanagan (both Lahinch), and Frank Flanagan (USA) (1996).

Miscellaneous articles and letters from the John Bhaba Jaick Ó Congaola collection: Ken Crotty, 'Sinking of Irish Boat Described' (3-10-1949) (Newspaper).

6. *Boston Irish Reporter*: 'Cohasset Monument Honors Famine Victims' (October 1996).

Brig St. John *of Galway was Cohasset's Worst Shipwreck*, Cohasset Historical Society. John Bhaba Jaick Ó Congaola collection.

Miscellaneous articles and letters from the John Bhaba Jaick Ó Congaola collection: Article by Robert N. Fraser, the Curator of the Cohasset Maritime Museum, (1-1-1979).

The Boston Daily Herald: 'The Burial of the Victims of the *St. John* – Melancholy Sight' (12-10-1849).

The Patriot Ledger: 'Ceremonies to Honor Irish Shipwreck Victims' (6-10-1999).

Chapter VII

1. *Boston Irish Reporter*: 'Cohasset Monument Honors
   Famine Victims' (October 1996).
   Brig St. John *of Galway was Cohasset's Worst Shipwreck*,
   Cohasset Historical Society. John Bhaba Jaick Ó
   Congaola collection.
   Diary of Elizabeth Lothrop (11-10-1849, 25-12-1849).
   Ennistymon Parish Magazine, 'The Shipwreck of the *St.
   John*'. Article compiled from material supplied by Brud
   Slattery, John Flanagan (both Lahinch), and Frank
   Flanagan (USA) (1996).
   The Galway Vindicator: 'Awful Shipwreck at Minot's
   Ledge – Loss of *St. John* of Galway. About One Hundred
   Drowned – Men, Women and Children' (3-11-1849).

2. *Boston Irish Reporter*: 'Cohasset Monument Honors
   Famine Victims' (October 1996).
   Brig St. John *of Galway was Cohasset's Worst Shipwreck*,
   Cohasset Historical Society. John Bhaba Jaick Ó
   Congaola collection.
   Comber, H., *The Book of Thomas J. Comber and Eliza
   Comerford* (n.d.). John Bhaba Jaick Ó Congaola collection.
   Ennistymon Parish Magazine, 'The Shipwreck of the *St.
   John*.' Article compiled from material supplied by Brud
   Slattery, John Flanagan (both Lahinch), and Frank
   Flanagan (USA) (1996).
   Miscellaneous articles and letters from the John Bhaba Jaick
   Ó Congaola collection: Article by Robert N. Fraser, the
   Curator of the Cohasset Maritime Museum (1-1-1979).

The Boston Irish Echo: Paddy Mulkerrins, 'More on the Ill-fated Brig, *St. John* – Remembers the *St. John*' (14-4-1984); Bill Loughran, 'More on the Ill-fated brig, *St. John*,' (14-4-1984); Paddy Mulkerrins, 'Survivors found' (letter to editor); Bill Loughran, 'The Ill-fated Brig *St. John*' (14-1-1984).

3. Diary of Elizabeth Lothrop (11-10-1849, 25-12-1849).

4. *Boston Irish Reporter*: 'Cohasset Monument Honors Famine Victims' (October 1996).
    Brig St. John *of Galway was Cohasset's Worst Shipwreck*, Cohasset Historical Society. John Bhaba Jaick Ó Congaola collection.
    Comber, H., *The Book of Thomas J. Comber and Eliza Comerford* (n.d.). John Bhaba Jaick Ó Congaola collection.
    Diary of Elizabeth Lothrop (11-10-1849, 25-12-1849).
    Ennistymon Parish Magazine, 'The Shipwreck of the *St. John*'. Article compiled from material supplied by Brud Slattery, John Flanagan (both Lahinch), and Frank Flanagan (USA) (1996).
    The Boston Sunday Globe: '150 Years Later, Honouring the Irish who Died at Sea off Cohasset Coast' (3-10-1999); 'Remembering the *St. John* Disaster of 1849' (3-10-1999); 'Those Known to Have Perished' (3-10-1999).
    The Galway Vindicator: 'Awful Shipwreck at Minot's Ledge – Loss of *St. John* of Galway. About One Hundred Drowned – Men, Women and Children' (3-11-1849).

5. *Boston Irish Reporter*: 'Cohasset Monument Honors
    Famine Victims' (October 1996).
    Brig St. John *of Galway was Cohasset's Worst Shipwreck*,
    Cohasset Historical Society. John Bhaba Jaick Ó
    Congaola collection.
    Ennistymon Parish Magazine, 'The Shipwreck of the *St.
    John*'. Article compiled from material supplied by Brud
    Slattery, John Flanagan (both Lahinch), and Frank
    Flanagan (USA) (1996).

6. *Brig* St. John *of Galway was Cohasset's Worst Shipwreck*,
    Cohasset Historical Society. John Bhaba Jaick Ó
    Congaola collection.
    The Boston Daily Herald: 'Brig *St. John* of Galway, Ireland,
    Lost October 7, 1849, at Cohasset'; 'List of Survivors
    and Drowned'; 'The Burial of the Victims of the *St. John*
    – Melancholy Sight' (12-10-1849).

Chapter VIII

1. *Boston Irish Reporter*: 'Cohasset Monument Honors
    Famine Victims' (October 1996).
    Brig St. John *of Galway was Cohasset's Worst Shipwreck*,
    Cohasset Historical Society. John Bhaba Jaick Ó
    Congaola collection.
    Miscellaneous articles and letters from the John Bhaba
    Jaick Ó Congaola collection: Bob Cuble, 'Irish, Past and
    Present, Found Tragedy and Hope'.
    The Boston Daily Herald: 'Brig *St. John* of Galway, Ireland,
    Lost October 7, 1849, at Cohasset'; 'List of Survivors

and Drowned'; 'The Burial of the Victims of the *St. John* – Melancholy Sight' (12-10-1849).
The Galway Vindicator: 'Awful Shipwreck at Minot's Ledge – Loss of *St. John* of Galway. About One Hundred Drowned – Men, Women and Children' (3-11-1849).

2. Thoreau, Henry David, *Cape Cod* (1865), pp. 14, 15.

3. *Boston Irish Reporter*: 'Cohasset Monument Honors Famine Victims' (October 1996).
    Ennistymon Parish Magazine, 'The Shipwreck of the *St. John*'. Article compiled from material supplied by Brud Slattery, John Flanagan (both Lahinch), and Frank Flanagan (USA) (1996).
    Thoreau, Henry David, *Cape Cod* (1865), p. 16.

4. Thoreau, Henry David, *Cape Cod* (1865), pp. 16, 17.

5. *Ibid.*, p. 18.

6. *Ibid.*, p. 20.

7. *Centenary Commemoration* (booklet) (21-8-1949).
    Brig St. John *of Galway was Cohasset's Worst Shipwreck,* Cohasset Historical Society. John Bhaba Jaick Ó Congaola collection.
    Ennistymon Parish Magazine, 'The Shipwreck of the *St. John*'. Article compiled from material supplied by Brud Slattery, John Flanagan (both Lahinch), and Frank Flanagan (USA) (1996).

Notes copied from Newcomb Bates (Jr), the Town Clerk of (Cohasset) (7-10-1849).

The Boston Daily Herald: 'Brig *St. John* of Galway, Ireland, Lost October 7, 1849, at Cohasset'; 'List of Survivors and Drowned'; 'The Burial of the Victims of the *St. John* – Melancholy Sight' (12-10-1849).

The Patriot Ledger: Edward Rowe Snow, 'Brig Wreck Killed 143 Off Cohasset' (6-10-1959); Laura Doherty, 'Celtic Cross: Cohasset's Memorial to a Shipwreck'; 'Ceremonies to Honor Irish Shipwreck Victims' (6-10-1999).

The Pilot: George E. Ryan, 'Wreck of Brig *St. John*' (October 1979).

Thoreau, Henry David, *Cape Cod* (1865), p. 20.

Chapter IX

1. Ancient Order of Hibernians in America, undated letter.

    Boston Irish Reporter: 'Cohasset Monument Honors Famine Victims' (October 1996).

    Brig St. John *Memorial Mass*, Ancient Order of Hibernians. Father John Murphy, Division 9, Plymouth (4-10-1997).

    Brig St. John *of Galway was Cohasset's Worst Shipwreck*, Cohasset Historical Society. John Bhaba Jaick Ó Congaola collection.

    Fraser, Robert, *Cohasset Vignettes* (1981).

    Diary of Elizabeth Lothrop (11-10-1849, 25-12-1849).

    Ennistymon Parish Magazine, 'The Shipwreck of the *St. John*'. Article compiled from material supplied by Brud

Slattery, John Flanagan (both Lahinch), and Frank Flanagan (USA) (1996).

Miscellaneous articles and letters from the John Bhaba Jaick Ó Congaola collection: 'Catholics to Honour Irish Immigrants Lost in Cohasset Shipwreck of 1849' (1949). Notes copied from Newcomb Bates (Jr), the Town Clerk of (Cohasset) (7-10-1849).

The Galway City Tribune; Tribune Extra: 'Galway Victims of a Major Tragedy' (27-11-1998).

The Galway Vindicator: 'Awful Shipwreck at Minot's Ledge – Loss of *St. John* of Galway. About One Hundred Drowned – Men, Women and Children' (3-11-1849).

The Irish Immigrant: 'Brig *Saint John* Anniversary' (13-12-1999); 'Ninety-Nine Irish Lives Lost in Brig *St. John* Shipwreck' (September 1999).

The Pilot: George E. Ryan, 'Wreck of Brig St. John' (October, 1979).

2. *Brig* St. John *of Galway was Cohasset's Worst Shipwreck*, Cohasset Historical Society. John Bhaba Jaick Ó Congaola collection.
   Diary of Elizabeth Lothrop (11-10-1849, 25-12-1849).

3. *The Galway Vindicator*: 'Awful Shipwreck at Minot's Ledge – Loss of *St. John* of Galway. About One Hundred Drowned – Men, Women and Children' (3-11-1849).

4. *Brig* St. John *of Galway was Cohasset's Worst Shipwreck*, Cohasset Historical Society. John Bhaba Jaick Ó Congaola collection.

Comber, H., *The Book of Thomas J. Comber and Eliza Comerford* (n.d.). John Bhaba Jaick Ó Congaola collection. Miscellaneous articles and letters from the John Bhaba Jaick Ó Congaola collection: Article by Robert N. Fraser, the Curator of the Cohasset Maritime Museum (1-1-1979).

Notes copied from Newcomb Bates (Jr), the Town Clerk of (Cohasset) (7-10-1849).

The Boston Daily Herald: 'Brig *St. John* of Galway, Ireland, Lost October 7, 1849, at Cohasset'; 'List of Survivors and Drowned'; 'The Burial of the Victims of the *St. John* – Melancholy Sight' (12-10-1849).

David Wadsworth, The Curator of the Cohasset Historical Society, 'Information relating to the "*St. John*" wreck', (8-3-1984). John Bhaba Jaick Ó Congaola collection.

The Pilot: George E. Ryan. 'Wreck of Brig *St. John*' (October 1979).

Ó Congaola, John Bhaba Jaick, 'The Wreck of the Brig *St. John*.'

5. *Boston Sunday Herald*: 'Cohasset Ceremony Recalls Shipwreck' (10-10-1999).

Fraser, Robert, *Cohasset Vignettes* (1981).

The Boston Daily Herald: 'Brig *St. John* of Galway, Ireland, Lost October 7, 1849, at Cohasset'; 'List of Survivors and Drowned'; Joe McLaughlin, 'Tell it to Joe – Monument to shipwrecked Irish' (8-7-1976).

The Boston Irish Echo: Paddy Mulkerrins, 'More on the Ill-Fated Brig, *St. John* – Remembers the *St. John*' (14-4-1984); Bill Loughran, 'More on the Ill-fated Brig, *St. John*'

(14-4-1984); Paddy Mulkerrins, 'Survivors Found' (letter to editor); Bill Loughran, 'The Ill-fated Brig *St. John*' (14-1-1984).

The Patriot Ledger: Edward Rowe Snow, 'Brig Wreck Killed 143 Off Cohasset' (6-10-1959); Laura Doherty, 'Celtic Cross: Cohasset's Memorial to a Shipwreck'; 'Ceremonies to Honor Irish Shipwreck Victims' (6-10-1999).

Article by Robert N. Fraser, the Curator of the Cohasset Maritime Museum, 1-1-1979.

6. *The Irish World and American Industrial Liberator and Gaelic American*: Frank Durkan, 'Death of a Famine Ship' (6-10-1984).

Article by Robert N. Fraser, the Curator of the Cohasset Maritime Museum, 1-1-1979.

The Patriot Ledger: Edward Rowe Snow, 'Brig Wreck Killed 143 Off Cohasset' (6-10-1959); Laura Doherty, 'Celtic Cross: Cohasset's Memorial to a Shipwreck'; 'Ceremonies to Honor Irish Shipwreck Victims' (6-10-1999).

The Pilot: George E. Ryan, 'Wreck of Brig *St. John*' (October 1979).

7. *The Boston Irish Echo*: Paddy Mulkerrins, 'More on the Ill-fated Brig, *St. John* – Remembers the *St. John*' (14-4-1984); Bill Loughran, 'More on the Ill-fated Brig, *St. John*' (14-4-1984); Paddy Mulkerrins, 'Survivors found' (letter to editor); Bill Loughran, 'The Ill-fated Brig *St. John*' (14-1-1984).

Ó Congaola, John Bhaba Jaick, 'The Wreck of the Brig *St. John*'.

Chapter X

1. Thoreau, Henry David, *Cape Cod* (1865), pp. 20, 21, 22.

2. *Brig* St. John *of Galway was Cohasset's Worst Shipwreck,*
   Cohasset Historical Society. John Bhaba Jaick Ó
   Congaola collection.
   Fraser, Robert, *Cohasset Vignettes* (1981).
   Miscellaneous articles and letters from the John Bhaba
   Jaick Ó Congaola collection: 'The President of Cohasset
   Central Cemetery Corporation' (26-5-1914); 'Catholics
   to Honour Irish Immigrants Lost in Cohasset
   Shipwreck of 1849' (1949); 'The Wreck of the Brig *St.
   John*'.
   The Boston Daily Herald: 'The Burial of the Victims of the
   St. John – Melancholy Sight' (12-10-1849).
   The Galway Vindicator: 'Awful Shipwreck at Minot's
   Ledge – Loss of *St. John* of Galway. About One Hundred
   Drowned – Men, Women and Children' (3-11-1849).
   The Pilot: George E. Ryan, 'Wreck of Brig *St. John*'
   (October 1979).

3. *Centenary Commemoration* (booklet) (21-8-1949).
   The Pilot: George E. Ryan, 'Wreck of Brig *St. John*'
   (October 1979).

4. *Brig* St. John *of Galway was Cohasset's Worst Shipwreck,*
   Cohasset Historical Society. John Bhaba Jaick Ó
   Congaola collection.
   The Irish Emigrant: 'Brig *Saint John* Anniversary' (13-

12-1999). 'Ninety-Nine Irish Lives Lost in Brig *St. John*
Shipwreck' (September, 1999).

5. Miscellaneous articles and letters from the John Bhaba
   Jaick Ó Congaola collection: 'To Their Memory'.

List of Passengers and Crew

1. *Brig St. John of Galway was Cohasset's Worst Shipwreck,*
   Cohasset Historical Society. John Bhaba Jaick Ó
   Congaola collection.
   Miscellaneous articles and letters from the John Bhaba
   Jaick Ó Congaola collection: 'Wreck of the Brig *St. John*',
   1949.
   The Boston Daily Herald: 'Brig *St. John* of Galway, Ireland,
   Lost October 7, 1849, at Cohasset'; 'List of Survivors and
   Drowned'.
   The Boston Post: 'Brig *St. John* of Galway – List of
   Survivors and Drowned' (12-10-1849).
   The Galway Mercury: 'Wreck of an Emigrant Ship' (27-10-
   1849); 'Wreck of the *St. John*' (3-11-1849).
   The Galway Vindicator: 'Awful Shipwreck at Minot's
   Ledge – Loss of *St. John* of Galway. About One Hundred
   Drowned – Men, Women and Children' (3-11-1849).

2. *Brig* St. John *of Galway was Cohasset's Worst Shipwreck,*
   Cohasset Historical Society. John Bhaba Jaick Ó
   Congaola collection.
   Miscellaneous articles and letters from the John Bhaba Jaick
   Ó Congaola collection: 'Wreck of the Brig *St. John*' (1949).

The Boston Daily Herald: 'Brig *St. John* of Galway, Ireland, Lost October 7, 1849, at Cohasset'; 'List of Survivors and Drowned'.

The Boston Post: 'Brig *St. John* of Galway – List of Survivors and Drowned' (12-10-1849).

The Galway Mercury: 'Wreck of an Emigrant Ship' (27-10-1849); 'Wreck of the *St. John*' (3-11-1849).

The Galway Vindicator: 'Awful Shipwreck at Minot's Ledge – Loss of *St. John* of Galway. About One Hundred Drowned – Men, Women and Children' (3-11-1849).

The Irish World and American Industrial Liberator and Gaelic American: Frank Durkan, 'Death of a Famine Ship' (6-10-1984).

3. *Brig* St. John *of Galway was Cohasset's Worst Shipwreck*, Cohasset Historical Society. John Bhaba Jaick Ó Congaola collection.

   The Boston Daily Herald: 'Brig *St. John* of Galway, Ireland, Lost October 7, 1849, at Cohasset'; 'List of Survivors and Drowned'.

   The Boston Post: 'Brig *St. John* of Galway – List of Survivors and Drowned' (12-10-1849).

   The Galway Mercury: 'Wreck of an Emigrant Ship' (27-10-1849); 'Wreck of the *St. John*' (3-11-1849).

   The Galway Vindicator: 'Awful Shipwreck at Minot's Ledge – Loss of *St. John* of Galway. About One Hundred Drowned – Men, Women and Children' (3-11-1849).

4. *Brig* St. John *of Galway was Cohasset's Worst Shipwreck*,

Cohasset Historical Society. John Bhaba Jaick Ó
Congaola collection.

Diary of Elizabeth Lothrop (11-10-1849, 25-12-1849).

The Boston Daily Herald: 'Brig *St. John* of Galway, Ireland,
Lost October 7, 1849, at Cohasset'; 'List of Survivors and
Drowned'.

The Boston Post: 'Brig *St. John* of Galway – List of
Survivors and Drowned' (12-10-1849).

The Boston Irish Echo: Paddy Mulkerrins, 'More on the
Ill-fated Brig, *St. John* – Remembers the *St. John*' (14-4-
1984); Bill Loughran, 'More on the Ill-fated Brig, *St. John*'
(14-4-1984); Paddy Mulkerrins, 'Survivors Found' (letter to
editor); Bill Loughran, 'The Ill-fated Brig *St. John*' (14-1-
1984).

The Galway Mercury: 'Wreck of an Emigrant Ship' (27-10-
1849); 'Wreck of the *St. John*' (3-11-1849).

The Galway Vindicator: 'Awful Shipwreck at Minot's
Ledge – Loss of *St. John* of Galway. About One
Hundred Drowned – Men, Women and Children' (3-
11-1849).

5. *Brig* St. John *of Galway was Cohasset's Worst Shipwreck*,
Cohasset Historical Society. John Bhaba Jaick Ó
Congaola collection.

Ennistymon Parish Magazine, 'The Wreck of the Irish
Emigrant Ship', 'The Shipwreck of the *St. John*'. Article
compiled from material supplied by Brud Slattery, John
Flanagan (both Lahinch), and Frank Flanagan (USA)
(1996).

The Boston Daily Herald: 'Brig *St. John* of Galway, Ireland,

Lost October 7, 1849, at Cohasset'; 'List of Survivors and Drowned'.

The Boston Post: 'Brig *St. John* of Galway – List of Survivors and Drowned' (12-10-1849).

The Galway Mercury: 'Wreck of an Emigrant Ship' (27-10-1849). 'Wreck of the *St. John*' (3-11-1849).

The Galway Vindicator: 'Awful Shipwreck at Minot's Ledge – Loss of *St. John* of Galway. About One Hundred Drowned – Men, Women and Children' (3-11-1849).

6. *Brig St. John of Galway was Cohasset's Worst Shipwreck*, Cohasset Historical Society. John Bhaba Jaick Ó Congaola collection.

Diary of Elizabeth Lothrop (11-10-1849, 25-12-1849).

Ennistymon Parish Magazine, 'The Wreck of the Irish Emigrant Ship', 'The Shipwreck of the *St. John*'. Article compiled from material supplied by Brud Slattery, John Flanagan (both Lahinch), and Frank Flanagan (USA) (1996).

Miscellaneous articles and letters from the John Bhaba Jaick Ó Congaola collection: 'Wreck of the Brig *St. John*' (1949).

The Boston Daily Herald: 'Brig *St. John* of Galway, Ireland, Lost October 7, 1849, at Cohasset'; 'List of Survivors and Drowned'.

The Boston Irish Echo: Paddy Mulkerrins, 'More on the Ill-fated Brig, *St. John* – Remembers the *St. John*' (14-4-1984); Bill Loughran, 'More on the Ill-Fated Brig, *St. John*' (14-4-1984); Paddy Mulkerrins, 'Survivors Found' (letter to editor); Bill Loughran, 'The Ill-Fated Brig *St. John*' (14-1-1984).

The Boston Post: 'Brig *St. John* of Galway – List of Survivors and Drowned', 12-10-1849.

The Galway Mercury: 'Wreck of an Emigrant Ship' (27-10-1849); 'Wreck of the *St. John*' (3-11-1849).

The Galway Vindicator: 'Awful Shipwreck at Minot's Ledge – Loss of *St. John* of Galway. About One Hundred Drowned – Men, Women and Children' (3-11-1849).

The Irish World and American Industrial Liberator and Gaelic American: Frank Durkan, 'Death of a Famine Ship' (6-10-1984).

Epilogue

1. Thoreau, Henry David, *Cape Cod* (1865), pp. 5, 7, 8.

2. *Ibid.*, pp. 1, 8.

3. Diary of Elizabeth Lothrop (11-10-1849, 25-12-1849). Thoreau, Henry David, *Cape Cod* (1865), pp. 5, 8, 10.

REFERENCES

The Articles, Letters, Magazines and Newspaper records contained in the references, some of which are undated, are mainly from the John Bhaba Jaick Ó Congaola collection.

Miscellaneous Articles

Bob Cuble, 'Irish, Past and Present, Found Tragedy and Hope'.

'Catholics to Honour Irish Immigrants Lost in Cohasset Shipwreck of 1849,' 1949.

Cormac Ó Gráda, 'Ireland's Great Famine'.

'Cross is Monument to Irish'.

'Immigrants – Memorial at Cohasset Being Erected – Brig St. John Wrecked in 1849 on Minot's Ledge – Victims of the Disaster Numbered 99' (Newspaper article).

Ken Crotty, 'Sinking of Irish Boat Described' (3-10-1949).

M. Kennedy, 'The Winter Voyages of the Famine Ships, Cushlamachree and Londonderry'.

Martin P. Harney, SJ, 'A Tragic Episode of the Irish Famine Immigration'.

Martin P. Harney, SJ, 'The Storm of October 1849'.

Martin P. Harney, SJ, 'The Wreck of the Brig St. John'.

Notes copied from Newcomb Bates (Jr), the Town Clerk of (Cohasset) (7-10-1849).

The League of the Sacred Heart (Loyla Chapel B.C. High School); 'Brig *St. John* of Galway, Ireland Lost October 7, 1849, at Cohasset'.

'The Wreck of the Emigrant Brig "*St. John*" on October 7, 1849,' statement of lifeboat crew.

'To Their Memory'.

'Wreck of the Brig *St. John*' (1949).

Private Letters

Ancient Order of Hibernians in America (undated).

Ancient Order of Hibernians in America (undated).

Ancient Order of Hibernians in America (5-12-1941).

Ancient Order of Hibernians in America (30-11-1961).

Ancient Order of Hibernians in America (21-5-1962).

The Archbishop of Boston (10-3-1999).

Article by Robert N. Fraser, the Curator of the Cohasset Maritime Museum (1-1-1979).

Boston College High School, Press Release, 'Midnight Memorial Mass for Irish Victims of Brig "*Saint John*" off Cohasset', Fr Walter Martin (October, 1989).

'Brig *St. John*', John Bhaba Jaick Ó Congaola.

The Curator of the Cohasset Historical Society (23-7-1978).

The Curator of the Cohasset Historical Society (29-11-1989).

The Curator of the Cohasset Historical Society, 'Information Relating to the "*St. John*" Wreck', David Wadsworth (8-3-1984). John Bhaba Jaick Ó Congaola collection.

The Curator of the Cohasset Maritime Museum (17-12-1978).

The President of Cohasset Central Cemetery Corporation (26-5-1914).

'The Wreck of the Brig *St. John*', John Bhaba Jaick Ó Congaola (1999).

Cohasset Town Records, Book II, 1844-1865.

Diary of Elizabeth Lothrop: 11-10-1849, 25-12-1849.

Internet Articles

http://www.moytura.com/sligo1.htm
http://www.islayinfo.com/Exmouth-islay-tragedy.html
http://www.clarelibrary.ie/eolas/coclare/history/shipwreck_st_jo
http://www.clarelibrary.ie/eolas/coclare/history/stjohn_burials
http://www.clarelibrary.ic/eolas/coclarc/history/awful shipwreck.htm

Interview

John Bhaba Jaick Ó Congaola, 18-7-2008.

Lecture

'The Brig *St. John* Disaster 1849', John Bhaba Jaick Ó Congaola, 29-1-2007.

Lloyd's Register and Supplement

1845, 1846, 1847, 1850.

Historical Maritime Information: Merchant Shipping
Losses and Shipwrecks.

Magazines

Brig St. John *of Galway was Cohasset's Worst Shipwreck*,
Cohasset Historical Society. John Bhaba Jaick Ó
Congaola collection.

Brig St. John *Memorial Mass*, Ancient Order of
Hibernians. Father John Murphy, Division 9,
Plymouth, 4-10-1997.

Centenary Commemoration, 21-8-1949.

Cohasset Vignettes, Robert Fraser, 1981.

Ennistymon Parish Magazine, 'The Wreck of the Irish
Emigrant Ship', 'The Shipwreck of the *St. John*'. Articles
compiled from material supplied by Brud Slattery, John
Flanagan (both Lahinch), and Frank Flanagan (USA),
1996.

Glór na nOileán, 'An Brig *St. John*', Pádraig Ó
Maoilchiaráin.

Marine Disasters, 'II – The Wreck of the *St. John*', Willard
De Lue.

The Mariner, 'The History of Central Cemetery', David
Wadsworth. John Bhaba Jaick Ó Congaola collection.

Newspapers

Boston Daily Herald:
'Brig *St. John* of Galway, Ireland, Lost October 7, 1849 at
Cohasset'.
'List of Survivors and Drowned'.

'Tell it to Joe – Monument to Shipwrecked Irish', Joe
    McLaughlin (8-7-1976).
'The Burial of the Victims of the *St. John* – Melancholy
    Sight' (12-10-1849).
'Triumph Out of Tragedy – Commemorating the 150
    Anniversary of the Great Hunger' (26-6-1998).

Boston Irish Reporter:
'Cohasset Monument Honors Famine Victims' (October,
    1996).

Boston Sunday Herald:
'Cohasset Ceremony Recalls Shipwreck' (10-10-1999).

Cohasset Mariner:
'Meeting the Governor' (2-7-1998).

Dublin Evening Post:
A report (9-9-1845).

Galway Advertiser:
'The Workhouse' (3-3-1994).
'When Galway Starved' (27-6-1996).

Galway Mercury and Weekly Connaught Advertiser:
A report dated 5-6-1847.
'A Famine Report' (13-3-1847).
'Emigration' (1-5-1847).
'Irish Sufferings – Whig and Tory Sympathy' (3-7-1847).
'More Deaths by Starvation' (22-1-1848).

'Passage Across the Atlantic' (19-6-1847).
'Song of the Famine' (5-9-1846).
'Starvation – Inquest' (13-3-1847).
'The Devon Commission' (26-6-1847).
'The Song of the Famine' (10-7-1847).
'Wreck of an Emigrant Ship' (27-10-1849).
'Wreck of the *St. John*' (3-11-1849).

Galway Vindicator:
'Awful Shipwreck at Minot's Ledge – Loss of *St. John*
    of Galway. About One Hundred Drowned – Men,
    Women and Children' (3-11-1849).

Illustrated London News:
A report dated 8-5-1847.
'Famine and Starvation in the County of Cork' (16-1-1847).
'Mortality in Skibbereen' (30-1-1846).
'Sketches in the West of Ireland', Mr James Mahony
    (13/20-2-1847).
'The Galway Starvation Riots' (25-6-1842).
'The Late Food Riots in Ireland' (7-11-1846).
'The Potato Disease' (18-10-1845).

The Boston Irish Echo:
'More on the Ill-Fated Brig, *St. John* – Remembers the *St.
    John*,' Paddy Mulkerrins (14-4-1984).
'More on the Ill-Fated Brig, *St. John*,' Bill Loughran (14-
    4-1984).
'Survivors Found', Paddy Mulkerrins (letter to editor).
'The Ill-Fated Brig *St. John*,' Bill Loughran (14-1-1984).

The Boston Mail:
'Wreck of the *St. John*' (11-10-1849).

The Boston Post:
'Brig *St. John* Memorial' (12-10-1849).
'Brig *St. John* of Galway – List of Survivors and Drowned'
(12-10-1849).
'The Burial of the Victims of the *St. John* – Melancholy
Sight' (12-10-1849).

The Boston Sunday Globe:
'150 Years Later: Honouring the Irish who Died at Sea off
Cohasset Coast' (3-10-1999).
'Remembering the *St. John* Disaster of 1849' (3-10-1999).
'Those Known to Have Perished' (3-10-1999).

The Connacht Tribune:
'The Great Famine, Tribune Extra' (24-3-1995).

The Freeman's Journal:
'The Burial of the Victims' (26-10-1849).
'The Wreck of the Irish Emigrant Ship *St. John*' (26-10-1849).
'Wreck of the Irish Emigrant Ship Lamentable Loss of
Life' (24-10-1849).

The Galway City Tribune; *Tribune Extra*:
'Galway Victims of a Major Tragedy' (27-11-1998).

The Irish Emigrant:
'Brig *Saint John* Anniversary' (13-12-1999).

'Ninety-Nine Irish Lives Lost in Brig *St. John* Shipwreck'
(September, 1999).

*The Irish World and American Industrial Liberator and Gaelic
American*:
'Death of a Famine Ship', Frank Durkan (6-10-1984).

The Jesuit or Catholic Sentinel:
'Memorial to Irish' (4-1-1934).

The Patriot Ledger:
'Brig Wreck Killed 143 off Cohasset', Edward Rowe Snow
(6-10-1959).
'Celtic Cross: Cohasset's Memorial to a Shipwreck', Laura
Doherty.
'Ceremonies to Honor Irish Shipwreck Victims' (6-10-
1999).
'Cross Monument to Irish', Edward Rowe Snow (6-10-
1959).
'Doomsday at Little Harbor', Bob Cubie (6-10-1999).
'Shipwreck Revisited: 99 Irish Immigrants Perished in
1849 Storm', Molly Hochkeppel (9-10-1989).
'To Mark Anniversary of Old Brig's Sinking', Edward
Rowe Snow.

The Pilot:
'Wreck of Brig *St. John*', George E. Ryan (October, 1979).

Tribune Extra:
'Galway Victims of a Major Tragedy' (27-11-1998).

Video

Brig *St. John.* Telegael.

BIBLIOGRAPHY

Comber, H., *The Book of Thomas J. Comber and Eliza Comerford* (n.d.).

Cunningham, J., *'A Town Tormented by the Sea': Galway 1790–1914* (Geography Publications, Dublin, 2004).

Gallagher, T., *Paddy's Lament, Ireland 1846-1847: Prelude to Hatred* (Poolbeg Press Ltd, Swords, 1985).

Garvey, Fr G., *Bushypark Celebrates 1837-1987* (Fr Gerard Garvey, 1988).

Henry, W., *Role of Honour, Mayors of Galway City 1485-2001* (Galway City Council, 2001).

Henry, W., *St Clerans: The Tale of a Manor House* (Merv Griffin, 1999).

Laxton, E., *The Famine Ships; The Irish Exodus to America 1846-51* (Bloomsbury, London, 1996).

Litton, Helen, *The Irish Famine: An Illustrated History* (Wolfhound Press, Dublin, 1994).

McBride, D., *When Hunger Stalked the North* (Adare Press, Banbridge, 1994).

Murray, J.P., *Galway: A Medico-Social History* (Kenny's Bookshop and Art Gallery, Galway, 1994).

Ó Cathaoir, Brendan, *Famine Diary* (Irish Academic Press, Dublin, 1999).

O'Dowd, Peadar, *Down by the Claddagh* (Kenny's Bookshop and Art Galleries Ltd, 1993).

O'Dowd, Peadar, *Galway City* (Galway Corporation, 1998).

O'Dowd, Peadar, *The Great Famine and the West 1845-1850* (Galway Corporation, 1995).

Ó hÉideáin, E., *The Dominicans in Galway 1241-1991* (The Dominican Priory, Galway, 1991).

Porteir, Cathal (ed.), *The Great Irish Famine* (Mercier Press, 1995).

Thoreau, Henry David, *Cape Cod* (WW Norton and Company, New York, 1865).

Villiers-Tuthill, K., *Beyond the Twelve Bens: A History of Clifden and District 1860-1923* (Kathleen Villiers-Tuthill, 1990).

White, R., *1847 Famine Ship Diary* (Mercier Press, Cork, 1994).

Woodham-Smith, C., *The Great Hunger* (Harper and Row, United States, 1989).

ALSO BY
WILLIAM HENRY